Introduction

"Great minds discuss ideas, average minds discuss events, small minds discuss people." — Eleanor Roosevelt

And hollow minds discuss themselves.

I wrote this book to help others find a job. I am not going to try to out-intellectualize you — I mean outsmart you. I just want to show you a nice little road map covering all the bases within the employment process. From cradle to grave. I hate that term.

Anyway, this road map will be what you will need to do, step by step, to put yourself into the best position to get the career you wish to pursue. These ideas come from a recruiter's perspective. I have spent time in staffing and in human resources both as a contractor and permanent employee and learned a lot.

The thing I learned most from the inside is what hiring managers are thinking. What they are looking for in a candidate and, more specifically, what they're *not*. From what types of resumes are being looked at these days — and, yes, there are ways to easily get yours thrown into the trash, even if you have the skills, if you don't present them properly — to recruiter blacklists that can permanently take you out of the entire recruiting process for companies you may be targeting.

Some of the topics I cover may inspire additional research on your end. That would be nice. Some might lead to an entirely new way of setting priorities, developing and managing your schedule, making task lists and networking full time. That would be the goal. Some of this information may build you an entirely new perspective on your life. That would be flattering.

I'm not going to change your entire life with this book, as some career experts preach. I mean I will still be giving it a sincere chance.

Piggybacking (I hate that term) off that second notion, the goal is to recreate your way of living, because some of you might not know exactly what to do each day when 'you're not being told by some superior. Some of you are already taskmasters and already organize your daily routine on your calendars. That's half the battle. To those folks, this book will help with suggestions about what to plug into that eight hour day.

Enough with all these "I's" now. Let's 'get to you.

This book isn't going to do the job for you.

Like a screenplay, you have to find the right spot to begin your tale. Where in your life do we start? Some of you might be employed, pro-active job-seekers. Some of you might have just receiving their first pink slip after working at the same company for the last 30 years and can't face retirement yet. Let's cover everything.

Cheers,
Matt

A

Accepting Your Unemployment

"Our greatest weakness lies in giving up. The most certain way to succeed is always to try just one more time." — Thomas A. Edison

A common question for most people who find themselves at high risk of losing their jobs is, "Now What?" Not to worry though because that is normal. To beat this worry, you cannot just start acting frantic and sloppy. You must take calculated approaches such as updating your resume, putting together a plan for your daily duties and setting up strategies that will secure your next outcome.

Self-Doubt

It is normal for most folks to begin worrying once this change happens. Yes, you have bills to pay, a mortgage, a car loan. Perhaps you have kids in college. These are all real concerns, but don't let them make you just jump to the next job that comes along. Instead, make your decision after a thorough review of your economic situation and prospects.

Eliminating Excesses

Cutting back on expenses is of the hardest part of the process because it can directly correlate to self-defeat when your day-to-day function is now impacted. Your new normal sets it. Anything involving change usually scares people, especially in a time of crisis. It is easy to go into denial about your job security and financial matters, but to prepare for a job loss, you must address your expenses.

Figure out unnecessary costs, such as additional features on your cable services or cell plan. Think about things that usually go to waste, like not finishing food before its expiration date. Recognize your spending habits, break them down and adjust them where necessary. This may be overwhelming at first, but once you start, you will be eager to see where you can stop bad spending habits and save money.

Talk with your whole family about expenses that need to be spared until you're back in a more secure position. Look at your bank or credit card statement to see the last two months' spending. Some statements organize your spending history by type of expense. There are also programs like Quicken that help with budgeting and monitoring expenses.

Health Insurance

If you're unemployed or face a layoff soon, the thought of losing your health insurance can be especially frightening. Unfortunately, it can also be expensive and another thing to pay for just as your income is being cut.

There are options to keep health coverage, however. While you may be tempted to go without insurance now because of the cost, paying for an illness or accident without insurance can cost even more. It's better to pay for insurance, even if it's more than you paid while employed, than to risk having no coverage.

COBRA

If your employer has more than 20

employees and you're covered by the employer's health plan, they are required to offer you COBRA insurance (named after the Consolidated Omnibus Budget Reconciliation Act of 1985) for 18 to 36 months. With COBRA insurance, you continue the same health coverage you had as an employee. Any costs you have incurred in the calendar year are applied to your deductible, so you don't need to start over. Before you accept COBRA, research the cost and coverage alternatives. While it certainly is better than no health insurance, COBRA is expensive. Your monthly premium can be twice the amount you paid while you were employed.

For example, if you paid $300 a month for coverage before you were laid off, your employer paid the other half. With COBRA, you must pay the full amount—including what your employer used to pay—so it could cost you up to $600 a month. For more details about COBRA, visit *www.dol.gov/dol/topic/health-plans/cobra.htm.*

Insurance Cost Considerations

1. Check if a working spouse can add you to an existing health care plan. Even if it's not an "open enrollment" period, a job loss is a qualifying life event that allows you to add or change coverage quickly or immediately.

2. Compare the cost of that plan with the cost of your own COBRA coverage.

3. Consider the benefits, co-pay amounts, and deductibles on your spouse's plan. Even though the premium might be lower, you may pay more on his or her plan.

Insurance Coverage Alternatives

If you are healthy, consider downgrading your benefits to keep your premium manageable. Also, explore health plan alternatives:

1. States with competitive health insurance markets may have less-expensive options available. For example, in some states, BlueCross BlueShield offers inexpensive individual and family plans.

2. Check out *www.ehealthinsurance.com* to compare COBRA to other insurance company plans.

3. The government's alternative, *Healthcare.gov*, which offers subsidized coverage to eligible applicants, went in effect in 2013 under the Affordable Care Act.

Work With Your Assets

Even during a depression, employers are still hiring. One must identify his or her strengths, by either asking other around them that know them closely, performing a self-imposed SWOT analysis, etc. The harsh reality is that you may have to work within another field related to your current skill sets, relocate to a territory offering better employment options or returning to education to better enhance those skills that are missing. You may even start your own business.

Career Counseling

If you struggle with adjusting to unemployed life (job searching, cutting back expenses, etc.) or you feel lost in what direction to take your life, consider seeking the services of a professional life coach or psychotherapist. A good counselor can help you escape an emotional rut, help you recognize your personal strengths, and envision your true potential!

How to Cope with Job Loss

Losing a job can lead to negative feelings, such as inadequacy, embarrassment, insecurity and devastation. Recovery can take time, making it easy to become depressed or anxious. Learning how to cope with job loss is crucial for avoiding this. It can lead to an even better future, like undiscovered opportunities or a new career path that you may not have thought about otherwise!

Supportive Steps

1. Anxiety or depression can force uneasiness, but this can be your chance to discover your next career that will alternatively be a better choice than your last position.

2. Go through the emotions involved with the transition as they come. If you feel the need to cry, cry. That is normal. Let your emotions do what they do without trying to hide or force them away.

3. It's only a job. There will be others.

4. Relax with your family and try to complete house projects you never had time for while you take this time off. Try to enjoy it, because once the new position begins, it's back to the rat race.

5. Cut back on unnecessary spending!

6. Update your resume and enroll into classes that will help you stay up to date with your industry trends.

7. Start job-hunting.

Stress Relievers

Turning your negativity into something good can be tough, but you must try. You must get back to doing things that can help alleviate your mind's worries. Try to take up activities you like. Here are some ideas.

1. Pray or meditate
2. Communicate with others in the same boat as well as your loved ones for support
3. Quit your bad habits
4. Relax with your favorite book, movie or music
5. Play some sports or games that require physical and mental strength
6. Write a blog or diary to help express your feelings
7. Volunteer

Negative Emotions

For most of us, job loss has a devastating emotional impact. You may experience some of the following emotions.

1. Rejection, failure, or a sense that you did a poor job.
2. Embarrassment or weakened identity from no longer earning an income.
3. Anger towards yourself, your former employer, the situation, the economy, etc.
4. Fear or anxiety about the future, your career, your ability to pay immediate financial needs and provide for your family.
5. Depression, which can result in even more challenges for finding a new job. These can include changes in eating/sleeping habits, low energy, avoiding people, neglecting hygiene and

appearance.

      6. Stress over any or all of these emotions.

Dealing with Negative Emotions

Any of these feelings are a normal response to job loss, but you must decide how to handle them. If you recently lost your job, you will come across people who recently lost theirs too, which can cause more stress. Job loss is always occurring; you just did not notice because it did not affect you personally. Ignore the fact that people around you are unemployed. Focus on yourself. Everyone has lost a job at some point, so don't take it personally. You're not the only one, although it may feel like it now.

You must make a choice when you lose a job: dwell on it or move on. Choose to move on! Feel the pain and then do something about it. Get yourself recharged and head out in full gear for the next lucky employer to see your value. You may realize one day that this job loss is a blessing in disguise. Many times this is true! Everything happens for a reason. So if you lose your job, pick yourself up, dust yourself off, and get back out there!

Coping Strategies

If your job loss was because of performance, learn from it for your future employment. If it was a layoff, it was out of your control. Company reorganization can result in eliminated positions, and this can affect people who have been excellent employees.

      1. Acknowledge your emotions. Don't hide

them. Take a few days to relax, recover and regroup.

     2. Get support from friends, family and professional colleagues. Maintain the human contact and interaction like you had at work. Don't isolate yourself.

     3. Maintain a healthy diet and avoid alcohol and drugs.

     4. Maintain a positive attitude and receive positive outcomes. It's a cause-and-effect relationship. This will drive you to do better and go farther. Even if you did not get a job today, you may tomorrow!

     5. Finding a job is your full-time job now. Even after you do get a job, keep looking once in a while. Always keep your options open.

     6. If you feel depressed—increased anger, changes in sleeping or eating, hopelessness or sadness—for longer than a week, seek professional help.

     7. Networking is emotionally satisfying and the most effective job search technique. Instead of dwelling on your job loss, you are actively eliminating the cause of your stress. Networking gives you face-to-face human interaction, new friends, new conversation, information and insight!

     8. During your job-hunt, keep a calendar with your daily schedule. This really helps you organize, focus and execute your job search. Anything on paper (or one of the many digital calendar applications) is easier to follow than a schedule in your head. You will be prepared and looking forward to upcoming events and tasks.

Experiencing Multiple Layoffs

     Unfortunately, consecutive recent layoffs or

settling for a lower income are becoming more common nowadays. Many Americans have lost two jobs in the past two years. This includes more high-level executives and management people.

Those who have experienced multiple layoffs are usually willing to settle for less. With more executive-level employees losing their jobs, people with repeated layoffs have a harder time proving their worth to hiring managers. Many businesses view such individuals as lacking capability and integrity, rather than as victims of a recession. Recently, President Obama addressed this issue head on by spearheading an initiative to get large employers to pledge not to discriminate against the long-term unemployed.

An Interview About Anxiety

I was approached by a student at the University of North Carolina in Wilmington who is a senior at Isaac Bear Early College High School. Because she is technically a high school student, she is required to complete a graduation project. For this she was required to interview someone either in the field she is researching or someone with life experience with the issue she's facing. Her project is the psychological effects of unemployment and includes organizing a job fair for the unemployed. So she wanted to interview me on the stresses associated with work and job loss and the destructive qualities of mental health problems. Here are my corresponding answers to her questions:

1. *In your years of business have you seen the correlation between unemployment and mental health issues such as depression, or anxiety?*

I actually can speak from the heart here. I

once battled anxiety for four solid years after I was let go from a job in Los Angeles. I had relocated just a couple years prior and was trying to get my feet on the ground. As soon as we found our groove, my wife and I were laid off during the 2008 collapse. I was determined to feel better. To not let myself feel sorry for myself. To "get my stuff together" and clean up my act. No one was going to feel sorry for me. No one was going to just give me a break without my proving myself. I was determined to make something of myself.

2. *In my paper I am researching something that is called the cycle of unemployment.*

Basically, the hopelessness that involuntary unemployment creates can start a vicious cycle of rejection and continuing hopelessness.

Do you believe that a good outlook on unemployment can really impact the cycle of unemployment?

Always stay positive. Positivity is key. If your outlook every day is one of fear and angst, then you're letting them win. You're letting the negatives win. You can't start a day thinking weird thoughts and worrying about problems you can't control. Even some items within your control, but indirectly, i.e., paying bills. So start a roadmap. Develop a game plan. I had been laid off before, but this one hit my subconscious. This one took the cake. I decided to go into my own business and four years later I have never been happier.

3. *Are the debilitating effects of unemployment actually visible in the unemployed people that you see on a daily basis?*

Sure. You can tell when someone's worried or lacking sleep, etc. I try to tell my clients to get involved and get active. Donate some time, spend time with family and friends, go on a run and explore your parks. Take up paddle boarding. Whatever. But make yourself a routine and stick with it. You'll feel accomplished and your new "home office" might start looking more and more homey. It's crucial to get into a routine again. Although this routine will be guided by you, not your bosses.

4. *We always see the people who think that people are unemployed simply because they are lazy or irresponsible. Do you think society plays a major role in the emotional health of the unemployed?*

Sure. I always like to say, "Who cares?" and move on away from people who bring you down or have bad things to say about unemployed folks. Karma does come around, though, and job security is very insecure. So the naysayers might be on the other side of the tables someday. But keep moving and discard the haters. I remember when I was first self-employed, people would ask when I was going to get a job. I had to keep convincing them I was working. Eventually I was out of strength to convince, so I started going along with the jokes. In my mind I knew I was on the right track and I WAS WORKING. It was only a matter of time before those haters started to see some results. We live in a results-based society, one that asks, "What can you do for me today?"

5. *Many mental health disorders can only be cured by a professional. Do you think the lack of psychological care for the unemployed could be the major source of mental issues among the unemployed?*

I think people need to address their issues in any manner they can. I avoided pills, but took dearly to speaking to people close to me about my anxiety. It felt really good to get some of those conversations out. I think people need to research anything they can to help alleviate the stress in their lives and start taking action!

6. *Volunteering is proven to help reduce the symptoms of depression. Do you think that a certain amount of hours of community service should be required for the unemployed?*

Absolutely! It feels wonderful helping those who are less fortunate. I always say there's always someone worse off out there. This rings true when you're working with the folks most in need. Strike up some conversation with them. Make THEM feel good. Trust me, you will too afterwards.

7. *Unemployment has been a hot topic for many years. Do you think the government could be doing more to aid the unemployed or should they leave it to the individual to get help?*

I think the government did a fine job back in 2008 when handling the colossal unemployment claims from the financial crisis. They actually extended a lot of folks up to 99 weeks. Now we obviously couldn't afford to keep doing that, but the government does assist in tremendous ways. I think it should fall on the previous employer. They laid you off and they should be the ones supplying outplacement so you can "get help." A career coach can be very helpful in understanding your burdens. A coach can also help you identify the new avenues to pursue once you start your job-hunt.

8. *Do you think mental health issues could be a major cause for long-term unemployment?*

I think it's a case-by-case scenario. Some people have trouble landing new jobs because their skills aren't what they need to be. Others don't interview as well. Some have other issues coming to light during this transition because of the "new normal." Everyone is different. So for me to say YES, mental health causes longer unemployment, is not accurate. I can tell you mental health issues definitely weigh down job-hunters. They wake up already burdened and weighed down psychologically. That's why they need to focus on the smaller items, one day at a time, systematically completing each task.

9. *Learning a new skill is fulfilling and exciting. Do you think certain classes, specialized for the unemployed, could help end the depression that comes with unemployment?*

Sure. Changes always spark new feelings of self-involvement. People battling mental health issues need that feeling of being grounded. That feeling of self-worth. That feeling that they can get excited and passionate again about something, anything! I not only think it's very beneficial to tackle a new trade or skill, but it should be apart of your long term game plan if searching for current work matching current skills is not generating results.

10. *Understanding of certain mental health issues is confused by useless drug commercials and ridiculous myths. Do you think providing the unemployed with the information that they need to combat diseases like depression or anxiety could potentially reduce the chance of them falling victim to the diseases?*

Sure. People battling health issues need the truth. They need to surround themselves with honesty and sincerity. It's imperative! I think the more truthful knowledge, the better. To combat the myths, I think they should focus their time on researching data from credible sources like The National Institute of Mental Health (NIMH) or *www.MentalHealth.gov.*

Remedies for Repeat Job Loss

    1. Attend training to refresh outdated skills

    2. Consider a new location, industry or profession

    3. Keep your best contacts in the loop about your job-hunt and make sure they have the latest version of your resume

    4. Send expert tips, information and newsletters on topics you know well to potential employers. Offer to take questions or give advice as a virtual consultant.

    Reference: See Chapter O, Online, for how you can use Twitter and Facebook for this.

    1. Create a personal website focused on potential employers*

    2. Use an outplacement service or career coach, like you are now!

    *A customized web page (on your website) highlighting your relevance to a specific company is a great way to attract attention. Give hiring managers a private link to this web page, for that company's eyes only! Describe how your experience would benefit their particular business and the issues it faces.

Fighting the Stigma

    You can fight the stigma of back-to-back layoffs by giving a sincere explanation during interviews: "I have been laid off twice in the worst economy in 50 years."

    Before starting your job-hunt, you must

overcome any anger about your recurring joblessness. If you have negative feelings, those emotions are reflected in your job interviews. Don't sound desperate, but be positive and enthusiastic!

Try helping the less fortunate to neutralize such negative feelings during your job search. Charity efforts can tap into your key skills, such as project management, networking, marketing, organizing, etc, and rebuild confidence. They are a great resume builder, too! Volunteer work shows you are doing something productive—in addition to other job-hunting tasks—during your time out of work.

Find a volunteer activity involving a company where you want to work. Your participation allows you to network with employees and a get a sense of whether you fit into their culture. In making this effort to understand a possible employer, talk with vendors, competitors and former employees. Use this research to give you insight so you can intelligently discuss the company's challenges when interviewing.

Surviving Multiple Interviews

One challenge for victims of multiple recent layoffs is surviving multiple interviews. As the applicant pool gets smaller with each round, people with recent repeat layoffs may be at a disadvantage.

Make a point of telling interviewers about your skills that are better than others, or that others don't have! For example, you might emphasize your frequent international business trips. Supply details about your work with managers in various countries and how you have customized your work to suit local culture and market conditions.

Persevere! Even if you are turned down, stay positive and keep pressing on with your job search. Stay in touch with all potential employers. Circumstances may change for the hiring manager. For example, the person hired instead of you ended up not taking the job, or didn't work out.

Finding Help

Getting laid off may require using state services you have never used before. Here are some starting places for finding help. (Most of the websites below are for North Carolina. Do an online search to find corresponding websites for your state.)

Am I eligible for unemployment insurance benefits?

If you have lost your job through no fault of your own, you may be eligible. Visit your state's Employment Security Commission website. For example, North Carolina's is: *www.ncesc.com/individual/UI/UiClaims2.asp*

How do I file for unemployment insurance benefits?

There are three options:
1. Online: *www.ncesc.com/individual/webInitialClaims/applyBegin.asp?init=true*
2. By telephone: 1-877-841-9617 (toll free, 24 hours a day, seven days a week)
3. In person: At your nearest Employment Security Commission (ESC) office *www.ncesc1.com/locator/locatormain.asp*

How do I start my search for a new job?

While a newspaper provides lots of independent job-seeking ideas, your local state unemployment office and JobLink Career Center staff can help you locate new employment possibilities and prepare to apply for jobs.

Find your nearest Career One Stop location at: *www.careeronestop.org*

I need training to move into a new career, but how can I pay for training without a job?

Look for opportunities within your community and visit these websites:

Apprenticeships:
www.nclabor.com/appren/appindex.htm
Financial aid:
www.cfnc.org
Free online training:
www.gcflearnfree.org
www.microsoft.com/ElevateAmerica
Service obligation loans:
www.cfnc.org/paying/schol/info_career.jsp
Trade Adjustment Act:
www.ncesc.com/individual/training/TAA.asp
Workforce Investment Act:
www.nccommerce.com/en/WorkforceService s/FindInformationForIndividuals/DislocatedWorker Toolkit/EmploymentTraining

B

Beginning Your New Phase in Life

"I believe in the dignity of labor, whether with head or hand; that the world owes no man a living but that it owes every man an opportunity to make a living." — John D. Rockefeller

No one cares that you're unemployed! That's a scary thought, huh? It sounds bad, but it's the truth. You have to get into the mindset that no one feels bad for you because you're unemployed, besides maybe your family and friends. So step one in your career search is to get over any idea that the next company "owes" you something. People just like you are out there looking for work and most likely went through the same layoff you did. Now that's a comforting thought. Remember, though, that those same people are your competition! Competition breeds confidence, thus you must have the confidence to learn or demonstrate the ability to help the employer's bottom line better than the next guy. That's what employers are searching for these days. They want someone who can improve the bottom line. They want to know what you can do for them.

Here's an important motivation to stop relying on employers: have the mentality that you only live once, so you need to make it good. Work hard every day! You can make it on your own. And while these are good principles to live by, the truth is that you do still need to rely on somebody: some place that will hire you. (That's true unless you choose to go into a form of entrepreneurship, and if that's the case, this book probably won't help much.

This information is meant to assist those seeking a career path within an organization.) Relying on an employer poses another problem, though. That's because companies don't have to hire you, but rather your "type," just a body that fits their requirement or job opening. You may have the best background and skills to fill a job, but the companies see your "type" over and over through its pile of resumes. What the company can do now is stay competitive, which means finding the applicant who has worked for a competitor or at least in the same industry, doing the exact same job as the one they're trying to fill.

After the company finds that exact match, it looks at two or three more items. Those would be, in this exact order: 1. How much will you cost? 2. Do you job hop? The third item would be education, if it's a company requirement. If you are an engineer, you will need at least a 'bachelor's degree in engineering to stay alive in this job market. I'll reiterate: the top three things an employer wants to know are your background relating to the job or industry, your price, and your work history, measured in years of employment. Employers want to see at least three years of successful employment with each company on your resume. The more the merrier. That means the key to future success is to stay with the company for a while once you do get a shot. Don't quit just because you don't get along with your boss right away or because you don't get what you want. Take advantage of your situation and count your blessings once you land a job,. The truth is that companies don't care about their employees as much as they used to. You never know when your ride in to work will be your last. You'd be extremely lucky and among a rare few if you were to stay with an organization long enough to earn a "gold watch" or a pension. Heck, you'd be lucky to stay with a company for more than five years! So consider it a success if you reach your five-year anniversary. Go buy yourself a nice lunch that day. I'll elaborate on this topic in later chapters.

Finding a Job is a Job in and of Itself

Did you spend eight hours today looking for a job? Did you spend eight hours networking, going to interviews or branding yourself? Did you spend eight hours doing anything to advance you into your next job? If not, why? Your competition is doing these things. Every day should be used as a "work" day even if you aren't technically working at an office or on the road for a company or as a business owner. You need to make job-hunting your number one priority. The more you put yourself out there, the higher the chances of being seen and thus landing an interview. Remember, it takes work to get work. Don't wait until your severance pay or unemployment benefits run out! Start now.

Ways to Make Your Job Search a Full-Time Job

1. Stick to a daily schedule. Create a to-do list and cross tasks off as you go; this gives you a sense of accomplishment even during down times.

2. Check job boards daily and see if any new jobs were posted, just in case your alert notification services have missed anything.

3. Send printed resumes by mail. Few people do this anymore, which is why it will be effective for you.

4. Target companies you want to work for, where you know you can add value, then network or market yourself into an interview.

5. Contact recruiters and temporary work agencies. Recruiters work for you. The good ones don't charge you to help find you employment. However, don't constantly bug recruiters. If they need someone with your skills, they will call you. They might not have an opening right away that fits your qualifications, but if they do, they will call you.

6. Apply only to the openings that fit within your area of expertise. Recruiters do get "jack of all trades" candidates who, in actuality, only fit the bill for one or two jobs at most. So be aware of resume where you're submitting your resume. Don't try to market yourself as a "jack of all trades" or a "fast learner." Do market yourself as an expert in a particular industry or field. Hiring managers aren't going to take the time to figure out where you might fit. They want to know whether you fit their immediate need.

7. Apply to higher positions than what you now hold. For your next job, why not go from a rank-and-file worker to a manager? If you are an exempt or professional worker, set your sights high and become a leader.

8. Follow the job posting directions and make sure you do what they tell you to do. Employers specify rules for a reason.

9. Read industry magazines, blogs and websites. Keep up with trends and developments in your field.

10. Network with industry experts and other people who can help you find a job. Create your own advisory board to consult with when you need information or assistance.

11. Create an online presence. Sign up for industry blogs, social networking sites and career

sites.

12. In a worst-case scenario, be flexible about relocating. It is an unavoidable part of job-hunting these days.

Right Place, Right Time, Right Person

Right place: Any place can be the right place, so make the most of where ever you are. An interview, career fair, career mixer, even the grocery store can be a networking opportunity that can turn into a new job or career.

Right time: It is always the right time. Whether or not they are hiring or advertising a position, network with company decision makers.

Right person: Find the top 10 companies you want to work for and list them in priority order. Research each company's senior management on LinkedIn and Google. Contact them via LinkedIn or their company email, or call the company and ask to speak to them directly.

If you reach someone who can tell you what the hiring manager is looking for, ask:

1. What are they looking for in a candidate?

2. What are they definitely not looking for?

3. What turns them off about a candidate?

4. Are they having any issues in filling this position?

Once you reach the hiring manager, give him or her your elevator speech. It is very difficult because you are writing—a resume, cover letter or email—or talking to someone you don't know. So every message must be customized for the position the company is filling! See the section on Self-Marketing in Chapter D for more about elevator speeches.

Some Reality Checks

1. Here's some bad medicine. Sometimes you have to take a step down, relocate to a better area for your particular position, or even take a pay cut. Make the assessment and be honest with yourself and anyone else this will be affecting. Relocating is a part of job-hunting these days and you need to be flexible in worst-case scenarios.

2. A good tip is to know what you want, immerse yourself in all you can within that industry—keeping up with trends, reading industry blogs and magazines—and becoming an expert. This will ensure you're able to take on increasing responsibility, which in turn will increase your paycheck. This will also help you avoid doing the typical things everyone else in that industry is doing to get a job!

3. Reject mediocrity and overcome setbacks. Lay out your passions and the things that motivate or excite you. Then pursue them with all you've got!

4. Increasing your responsibility will increase your pay. Your paycheck will increase only through increasing responsibility

5. People tend to analyze celebrities or elite people and try to guess what they're thinking at certain points in their life. This could be during a game for an athlete, during a meeting for a CEO, or while working on a book or on a set for an author or actor. We try to either imitate them or at least try to understand what they're thinking so we can understand them better.

6. Knowing what you want and not doing what everyone else is doing will help you stand out in this competitive world.

7. Help others out! Why? Because we're all

in this together! Share your expertise!

8. If you've lost your job, stay positive. Remember, many people out there are in the same boat as you. Most likely a lot of them are a lot worse off than you, too.

9. Another great source is to network with your local Department of Labor, and the local outplacement coordinator or workforce specialist.

Some Advice from the Pros

A few hard truths and statements from hiring managers and recruiters are below. Several of them touched on nuances that stuck out during the hiring process. I thought this hit home. A couple of these nuggets might help you out, too.

1. Some recruiters will not consider your credentials if you are out of work for over seven months.

2. Who you know does make a difference on your job search.

3. Target hiring managers over recruiters and HR employees.

4. I never read cover letters.

5. Pick a smartly chosen email address to use for resume submissions.

6. Do not put your graduation date on your resume if you have been out of school for over 25 years.

7. Don't reduce text size on your resume. People won't waste time squinting to read your information.

8. Don't make your resume past two pages. You can tell your story in two pages.

9. Write words directly into your resume that are on the job description, so the tracking system will select your resume based on those

keywords.

10. Don't put color on your resume unless you are in a creative industry or position.

11. Research the company before the interview.

12. Overweight people can have a harder time finding employment.

13. Don't bring your cell phone to the interview because it's a distraction and it might go off during the interview (we all sometimes forget to mute it).

14. Greet interviewers with a firm handshake and smile.

15. Let the interviewers talk as much as they want and just listen. This builds rapport.

16. Never negotiate a rate on the first interview, as you will get stuck with that salary for a long time.

17. Recruiters make money off of placing a candidate, so make sure you explain your financial preferences with them up front.

C

Career Fairs

"The way to get started is to quit talking and begin doing." — Walt Disney

Career Fair Techniques

Before the Fair

1. Get a list of employers appearing at the fair. Research the companies you want to see and learn as much as you can about them.
2. Prepare a list of employers you definitely want to approach.
3. Make sure your resume is ready. Bring different versions if you're targeting different jobs or industries.
4. Have your elevator speech ready. Practice it until you're comfortable using it and don't sound programmed.

At the Job Fair

1. Dress professionally, always, no matter what type of career fair.
2. Bring copious numbers of resumes. Better to have too many than not enough.
3. Bring a nice binder to store resumes. Include a notepad and pen to take notes or further directions from employers.
4. Go early if possible so you can avoid the rush! You can approach the recruiters while they are fresh.
5. Visit your lower-priority companies first.

This lets you practice your elevator speech with them to be sure you're ready for your top priority companies.

6. Don't wander around aimlessly and waste your precious time. Focus on your goals and follow your list of employers.

7. Make eye contact, shake hands firmly and create that good first impression with an employer.

8. Always maintain your professionalism. Employers notice everything!

9. Instead of waiting in long lines, network with other job-seekers and employers, even those not on your list. Anyone can help you find a job!

10. Be prepared to answer multiple questions in a short time with each employer. Act as if each conversation is an actual interview.

11. Ask questions only about the job and what the hiring managers are looking for. Wait until after the interview, or better yet do your homework in advance, to find out about the company.

12. Keep the conversation flowing, asking questions that are engaging and smart. Don't miss a chance to show how your skills and experience relate to the company or job opening.

13. Don't take up too much of anyone's time. Conclude with a thank you and move on. If you are interested and believe they are too, follow up soon after the job fair.

14. Always request business cards or at least write down contact information so you can follow up with a thank you and pursue any leads.

15. Listen to employers' instructions about your next steps. Take brief notes on the back of their business cards to help with follow-up.

After the Job Fair

     1. Keep yourself fresh in the mind of the decision makers. Sending a hardcopy follow-up or thank-you letter or (email is appropriate and quick) only taking a few days. Always refer to the specifics of the job fair. Try to mention any part of the conversation that stood out to make it easy for your contact to remember you. Inform the employer of your continued interest. Attach your resume.

     2. If the recruiter gave you specific application instructions, be sure to follow through as directed.

D

Defining Brand: You. Creating and Self-Marketing Yourself to Find Employment

"A company is no longer made up of anonymous people building one brand; rather, it is made up of many personal brands that are telling your one corporate-brand story in their own personal ways." — Mitch Joel, President, Twist Image; author of "Six Pixels of Separation." You can find him here: *www.twistimage.com/blog.*

Self-Marketing

Overview

A career brand is an image that portrays you as an expert in your field, attracts your ideal employer, and reveals how you can help an employer's business. How can you promote your career brand effectively, to stand out among increasing competition in the workforce? The answer is self-marketing!

Before you begin self-marketing, you need to understand:

1. What you're going to market about yourself
2. Who you're going to market yourself to
3. Why you're going to market yourself to your chosen prospects

This document offers some important tools to develop your career brand and understand your self-marketing plan.

Goals of Self-Marketing

This is what you should be trying to achieve:
1. Provide yourself direction to help eliminate trial and error. As a result, save time and money.
2. Network with key industry players.
3. Identify your transferable skills. Marketing these skills, not just your job history and accomplishments, puts you in higher demand, meaning you get more interviews.
4. Determine what other industries your transferable skills fit into. The industry you are in affects your career's success. Market yourself in growing industries, such as green-collar, biotechnology, nutrition and information technology. Steer away from dying industries like textiles, printing, newspapers or steel manufacturing.
5. Resolve any setbacks that hurt your career and prevent you from getting interviews. Fix your resume so it doesn't portray you as a "job hopper," "lacking education," or "unable to advance at a company."

Create Your Own Mission Statement

Just as mission statements provide direction and purpose for companies, individuals can benefit from having their own personal mission statement, too.
Your mission statement says what is important to you. Write yours before starting a career to get yourself on the right path. This will help you connect with companies that have similar values and beliefs. You can revise it or write a new one when you reach your next career crossroads. Its

sense of purpose is great motivation!

What to include:

1. Goals—Aspirations in life, both short-term and long-term

2. Core values—Who you are and what your priorities are

3. Successes—Professional, personal, etc.

4. Offerings—How you can make a difference for the world, your family, employer or future employers, friends and community

Integrate Assessments into Your Career Branding

Career and personality assessments help you to see the consistent patterns in your traits, characteristics, strengths, preferences, and skills. The results may lead you in a new career direction. If you have an established career, these assessments tell you how well your traits and branding messages align with your current career path.

Present your distinctive and noteworthy traits to your targeted employers. Remember that not all recurring patterns contribute to good branding. For instance, you wouldn't want to advertise a trait like introversion. Disregard any pattern that you feel isn't really you.

Incorporate the assessment results into your career branding materials. Those include resume, cover letter, elevator speech, interview responses, portfolio and business card. Convey a consistent branding message throughout all of these materials. But you can use different branding statements for different industries.

Tag! You Are 'It'!

Self-marketing is not just about selling your

specific skills. Everyone has skills. They get you in the door, but don't necessarily get you the job. Each job posting may get 100 or more applicants, and they all have the same or better skills than you do. How can you stand out as "the one"?

Here's how: develop a tagline. A great tagline tells people exactly what a product is and how they will benefit from using it. This is what employers want to know about you! Specifically, how you will help them make money and save money. Tell them how much money you helped a previous or current employer make or save on a particular project, sale, or time period.

Dear Career Journal:

Did you keep a diary or journal when you were young? It helped you express feelings when no one else would listen, or when you didn't want anyone else to listen! Similarly, a journal can help and guide you in your professional adult life too.

Writing in a career journal allows you to set aside time to think and learn more about yourself and your career. Just as when you were younger, keeping a journal allows you express emotions, good and bad, about your career progress. When you read past entries, you'll see how far you have come!

Use your career journal to:
1. Write your personal mission statement
2. React to self-assessment tests
3. Do a SWOT (Strengths, Weaknesses, Opportunities, Threats) analysis
4. Evaluate your current situation
5. Reflect on your successes and failures
6. Devise career goal ideas (breaking into a new career, as a volunteer or consultant)

7. Think about career alternatives

8. Establish daily or weekly career-related objectives or tasks

9. Develop action plans to achieve your objectives and tasks

10. Make checklists

11. Record network contacts, job interview results, etc.

12. Develop job correspondence material (cover letters, resumes, thank you letters, etc.)

13. Practice job interview questions and answers

14. Gather salary information

15. Jot down ideas and information you like and want to use in the future

16. Record things you want or need to learn, or skills to improve upon

17. Discover and explore your workplace values

18. Record your job-related likes and dislikes—and employers' likes and dislikes

19. Note lessons learned

20. Develop ways to improve the workplace

21. Review job-search trends

22. Develop plans for achieving promotions

23. Document the career paths of your peers whom you want to emulate

24. Prepare for job performance reviews

Don't keep your career journal at your workplace. Keep it at home, on your computer or in a notebook. Try to set a regular time of day to work on your journal, maybe right after work. Or maybe before work, to get yourself motivated and focused on what you can achieve during the work day!

Your journal is always ready, and no matter where your career path leads you, you can continue to use it throughout your professional life.

Key Marketing Tools

Strategic Marketing Plan

Your plan answers these questions:
1. What have I accomplished, where am I now, and where will my career be if I don't take action?
2. Where do I want to go with my career?
3. How do I get to where I want to go?
4. How do I put my plan into action?
5. What do I need to change if I'm not getting success?

Market Research

Understand trends in your career field. Consult resources such as the U.S. Department of Labor's Occupational Outlook Handbook. Interview industry professionals. Study the companies you would like to work for. Use this information for your cover letter, resume and job interview.

Marketing Mix

You are probably already familiar with the 4 P's of marketing, or the "marketing mix." The 4 P's are product, promotion, place, and price. Translate these in terms of yourself and your career for job search success.

Product. You are the product with unique characteristics, features, and skills. Highlight your "product features" in your tagline and resume. Let employers know your work experience, leadership experience, professional memberships, technical skills, education and training.

Make sure that your online marketing tools, such as Facebook or Twitter, are cleaned up and employer ready. You don't want a potential employer to see something on your personal networking sites that will land you in trouble.

Don't forget "packaging," to properly present yourself and your credentials to potential employers. Reference: See the "Dress for Success" section in Chapter K for dress guidelines. See Chapter R for resume best practices, and Chapter L for cover letters.

Promotion. This is your cover letter, resume, phone calls, correspondence and interviewing. Promotion tools include anything that you can use to get a job interview and ultimately get a job offer.

Be memorable by using multimedia marketing like email and follow-up phone calls. Or try using regular priority mail envelopes to send resumes, cover letters and other "marketing materials." This builds your career brand and increases your distinctiveness.

Place. This includes everywhere employers can access you. How are you reaching employers or people who can connect you with employers?

1. Internet job-searching and applying to job postings

2. Cold calling

3. Networking with current and former coworkers, colleagues and alumni

4. Speaking with recruiters at staffing and employment agencies and company HR departments

5. Visiting your university career centers and alumni offices

6. Attending professional association meetings and seminars

Price. This includes all aspects of the compensation you can receive from potential employers, as well as your strategies to get the price you want and that the employer feels you deserve. Your price not only includes salary, but also insurance, benefits, paid time off and perks.

Call in the SWOT Team!

Performing a SWOT Analysis, to be used in marketing planning, is a helpful exercise. SWOT stands for Strengths, Weaknesses, Opportunities, and Threats. It answers:

1. What are your strengths and weaknesses —in your internal environment?

2. What are opportunities and threats in your career field —your external environment?

Strengths

Internal, positive aspects that you can capitalize upon, such as:

1. Work experience
2. Education
3. Technical skills and knowledge, such as computer skills
4. Personal characteristics, for instance, a superior work ethic)
5. Strong network of contacts
6. Involvement with professional associations and organizations
7. Enjoying what you do

Weaknesses

Internal, negative aspects that you plan on improving, such as:

1. Lack of work experience
2. College major inconsistent with the job

you're looking for

3. Lack of specific job knowledge

4. Weak technical knowledge

5. Weak skills, such as leadership, interpersonal, communication, teamwork

6. Weak job-hunting skills

7. Negative personal characteristics, for example, lack of motivation, indecisiveness, and shyness

8. Weaknesses identified in past performance appraisals

Opportunities

External, positive conditions out of your control, but that you plan to leverage or add value:

1. Field trends that create more jobs (e.g., globalization, technology)

2. Field needs your set of skills

3. Opportunities for advancement in your field

4. Location

5. Strong network

Threats

External, negative conditions out of your control, but that you may be able to overcome:

1. Trends in the field that diminish jobs, such as downsizing or obsolescence

2. Companies aren't hiring people with your major or degree

3. Competition from recent college graduates with your same degree

4. Competitors with superior skills, experience or knowledge

5. Competitors who attended better schools

6. Limited advancement in your field—too competitive

7. Limited professional development in your field

8. Find hiring/employment trends in your field. Go online to ABI/INFORM, Business News Bank, and Lexis/Nexis.

After completing your SWOT Analysis, add the results to your Strategic Marketing Plan. Also, use your SWOT results to develop the following portions of your Plan:

1. Career goals

2. Marketing strategies

3. Action plan with deadlines

The Elevator Speech

The elevator speech is a clear, concise introduction that can be delivered in the time it takes to ride an elevator from the top to the bottom of a building. It can be as short as 15 seconds or as long as three minutes. Write down your elevator speech, and practice it so it comes naturally. Be ready to deliver it!

Use it at:

1. Networking events, including "unconventional" ones, like shopping

2. Career fairs

3. Cold calls to employers

4. Voicemails

5. Your current workplace, when you encounter the higher-ups

6. Job interviews, when you're asked, "Why should I hire you?" or "Tell me about yourself."

Your elevator speech includes:

1. A greeting

2. Your name

3. Your industry or field

4. Accomplishments, background, qualifications and skills

5. If you are graduating soon, what school and what degree

6. What you want to do and why

7. Why you enjoy what you do or want to do

8. What interests you about the listener's company or business

9. What sets you apart from others

10. Your tagline, which you developed!

11. Your mission statement, which you developed!

Finally, capture their interest and request action.

1. At a career fair: "May I have your business card, and give you my card and resume? Can you add me to your company's interview schedule?"

2. Networking: "What advice do you have for me? What employers do you suggest I contact?"

3. On a cold call: "When can we meet to discuss how I can help your company? May I send you my resume?"

Online Presence

Self-market online and search for networks you are familiar with, depending on your profession. Always be networking! Use the following sites for researching and networking with business professionals, including companies and employees:

1. ZoomInfo, *www.zoominfo.com*, business networking.

2. Facebook, *www.facebook.com*, social

networking.

3. iKarma, *www.ikarma.com*, business networking.

4. Sales Force, *www.salesforce.com*, sales leads and business networking.

5. LinkedIn, *www.linkedin.com*, business and employment networking.

6. Myspace, *www.myspace.com*, social networking.

7. NetworkingForProfessionals, *www.networkingforprofessionals.com*, business networking.

8. Ryze, *www.ryze.com*, business networking.

9. Spoke, *www.spokeo.com*, business white pages.

10. Twitter, *www.twitter.com*, social networking.

11. Xing, *www.xing.com*, business networking.

Career Assessments

Overview

A career assessment is typically done one-on-one with a counselor or coach. Career counselors who offer this service will have you answer a series of questions, which the counselor will use to offer specific advice to the job-seeker and impart techniques valuable to their job search. When a job-seeker knows exactly what career she wants and how to get it, her chances of getting interviews, and thus employment, will increase considerably. The goal is to help the job-seeker gain that insight via career assessments and feedback programs.

Career Aptitude Test

Finding a career that you'll enjoy can help you look forward to going to work every day. By recognizing and using your strengths, you can also open the door to professional opportunities. Career aptitude tests use a series of questions about your interests, hobbies, talents, what you enjoy doing, your style of working, and how you interact with other people. Remember, when taking a career aptitude test, it's important to be as honest as possible. Usually your first instinct is the right one. Your answers can help determine your skills and interests and find a career field that matches them. As you answer these questions, a career aptitude test can help you figure out your natural preferences and strengths. Aptitude tests then try to match these preferences and strengths with a large database of careers. An assessment test can't guarantee the perfect career—but it can be a wonderful tool to narrow down your choices or open up avenues you might never have thought to explore!

Guerrilla Marketing

As competition grows in this ailing economy, guerrilla marketing is a new alternative. Just make sure the culture of the company you're targeting accepts your methods. You want them to think you're clever and ambitious, not crazy! Think of original ways to market yourself creatively. You can get the job you want by not doing what everyone else is doing! Stand out!

These are some unconventional ideas to consider.

Billboards

Place your picture and a brief career summary on a billboard. Although expensive, it shows employers your creativity, passion and drive to land the perfect job.

Personal Resume Website

Create a website tailored towards your skills and resume. This can be very economical if done yourself, but the more elaborate and professional your site, the more it can cost. The chances of being found are growing as recruiters are using the Internet as a main search tool. Post a portfolio of projects you've worked on to show skills you can offer to a prospective employer. A link to your website is a natural extension of your resume.

Windshield Marketing

Distribute flyers on cars promoting yourself, your skill sets or your resume.

Java Marketing

Send the hiring manager a coffee cup and a coffee gift card with a note stating, "Let's get together to talk about the job position over coffee. I'll be calling soon." Send it via the Postal Service's registered two-day delivery option. Monitor the delivery through the *USPS.com* portal. After they sign for it, call in 20 minutes.

Donuts and Breakfast

Bring the office donuts or breakfast every Friday, specifically to the department where you want to work. They get to know you and your work ethic better. This is a popular practice clients and vendors use to stay fresh in the company's mind.

T-shirt Promotion

Use a single-shirt maker service, such as *Cafepress.com*, to create a piece of apparel that highlights your career assets and credentials

Sandwich Boards

Stand (or dance!) on a street corner with a sign presenting your credentials or career summary. Make sure you choose a corner that's both well-traveled and SAFE.

Blogs

Create a newsletter or blog and send articles to your network. Create an article on your expertise, so you can showcase this knowledge to everyone who reads it. You never know who will read it: such as a potential hiring manager! Some good blogging sites are Blogger, WordPress and Tumblr. It's a good idea to promote your expertise, not your availability. For instance, when engineers post comments on industry blogs that show their expertise, some of the readers may be decision makers. This sort of notice can lead to your next interview solely on an executive being impressed by your leadership and knowledge. You can also write articles in industry publications or try speaking on panels of experts at industry events. These tactics can also generate some residual income.

Summing Up Your Self-Marketing Plan & Career Brand

Your career brand, which you promote through self-marketing, includes the following:

1. Actions, attitude and appearance
2. Career assessment results
3. Personal mission statement
4. Elevator Speech
5. Tagline
6. Resume, cover letter, business card, etc.
7. Skills and education
8. Network of contacts
9. Online presence (LinkedIn, personal website, blog, job search engine profiles, etc.)
10. Industry presence (in professional associations, publications, speeches and presentations, awards or other contributions)

E

Experiential Learning

"Tell me and I forget. Teach me and I remember. Involve me and I learn." —Benjamin Franklin

Consider experiential, work-based learning to improve your knowledge of occupations that interest you. This can be done through internships, volunteering, part-time jobs, study abroad and more.

Gaining experience while exploring career options gives you a head start on your future career. Local schools and colleges offer many of these programs. Find more by searching the Internet and contacting businesses and organizations in your community.

Work-based learning is also beneficial if you want or need to change careers. Use your skills and gain new ones while building your job search network.

Participating in work-based learning opportunities gives you an edge when applying for jobs. Not only do you gain valuable work experience, but it offers a world of networking opportunities. Hiring managers always look favorably on this experience. If you have been recently laid off, this is a resourceful way to spend time away from work.

Internships

Internships allow you to observe and perform actual job duties that interest you, much like a regular employee. Companies usually provide interns more help and guidance while training and may also help them land a full-time job when the internship is completed. They may even provide a mentor who can support your career decisions and goals.

Employers like to hire people with experience, especially from within the company, and that includes their most successful interns. Internships are typically available to college students in a relevant major, but companies do hire non-students for internships.

Internships can be paid or unpaid and may be eligible for academic credit at a high school or college. They usually last for a couple of weeks to several months.

Cooperative Education

Cooperative education ("co-op") is on-the-job training within a higher learning institute. You do have the ability to apply some of this training towards your college credits. Each school is different, so you will need to look into your respective institution's guidelines.

Apprenticeships

These programs offer a combination of academic instruction, structured vocational training and paid work experience, usually lasting one to two years. These programs are offered through employers in collaboration with your state's department of labor and public school or community college system.

Apprenticeships are for skilled occupations, and are supervised by a master in the craft or trade. Relevant occupations are registered with your local division of apprenticeship and/or department of labor. North Carolina's is at *www.nclabor.com/appren/appindex.htm.*

As a candidate, you should tailor your search to what's in demand, if your career objectives allow for it. For example, heating and air conditioning seems to be an industry that continues to grow, and you can't outsource an HVAC mechanic! Same goes with the tool and die industry. Two years of pre-certifications and a year or two of training goes a long way. It's an investment. So try to learn a new passion for a field that's also hiring and paying these days, and make that investment to learn! Then you can take the basics and grow on the job. Know this: you are not going to start out at the top no matter what new industry your trying to learn.

Military members may be allowed to receive assistance with education. Visit www.gibill.va.gov for eligibility.

Job Shadowing

This is when you spend a day or part of a day at work with someone in a career that interests you. You follow that person throughout the workday and observe what tasks he or she performs and what skills are required for the job. You'll experience the work environment and interact with other people who work in your potential career field. It's a good idea to prepare by making a list of things you want to know about the job. At appropriate times during the day, ask questions about the work and make note of other questions that come up during the day. Job shadowing may not give you a complete picture of a job or career, but it at least gives you a sneak preview.

Volunteering

Volunteering is a good way to experience many careers. Volunteer opportunities are available everywhere: businesses, hospitals, schools, government agencies and community and nonprofit organizations. In some cases, you may be able to do the specific job that interests you. For jobs that require more education or training, ask the supervisor to place you in a related job that still exposes you to your career interests. Check for opportunities at your library and in your local newspaper.

Part-Time Jobs

Being underemployed seems to be a trend given the current state of the economy. Working teaches you a lot about your interests and helps you develop skills for many careers while earning some money for school and living expenses. Many part-time jobs don't require a lot of training or skill to get started. Part-time is typically considered anything less than 40 hours a week.

Education & Training Options after High School

These are indispensable avenues if you need further education or to strengthen your work knowledge and skills.

4-Year College

Get information about colleges and universities that meet your needs from your local library, school counselor or career center. Entrance requirements are primarily based on high school grades and college admission test scores. Contact the colleges directly or visit your local College Foundation. North Carolina's is *www.cfnc.org*.

Community College

Every state offers a variety of vocational and technical programs, lasting one semester to two years, to earn certificates, diplomas or associate degrees. They may also offer transfer programs and special training for your industry. They have open admissions, with remedial and pre-tech courses available. Entrance requirements depend on the program. North Carolina's website is *www.nccommunitycolleges.edu*.

Military

Joining the military allows you to get training, pay, room and board, and benefits. Ask your local military recruiter about types of training available, qualifications, length of commitment, pay and benefits. High school graduation is required.
1. Air Force: (800) 423-8723 (423-USAF) or *www.af.mil*
2. Army: (800) 872-2769 (USA-ARMY) or *www.army.mil*
3. Army National Guard: (800) 464-8273 (GO-GUARD) or *www.arng.army.mil*
4. Coast Guard: (800) 424-8883 or *www.uscg.mi*l
5. Marines: (800) 627-5637 (MARINES) or *www.usmc.mil*
6. Navy: (800) 872-6289 (USA-NAVY) or *www.navy.mil*

On-The-Job Training

Learn and earn by working for a company or business that trains you as you work. An internet search can help you find companies that offer training. During an interview, ask about programs for ongoing employee training.

Trade School

Check into learning a trade. There are numerous jobs out there that need able bodies and the only way to pursue the job is through proper trade school training. Tool and die makers and HVAC technicians are some of the careers needed in our economy that require proper training through a trade school. Both private trade schools and public community colleges offer such targeted vocational training.

F

Finding a Hiring Manager While Finding a Potential Employer

"When I have fully decided that a result is worth getting I go ahead of it and make trial after trial until it comes." — Thomas A. Edison

Researching a Prospective Employer

To write a customized resume and cover letter for a job position, you need to know about the company advertising it. Research to find out:

1. What does the company do?
2. How did the organization get started?
3. What are its products and services?
4. What are the company's plans?
5. Does it appear to be in good financial shape?
6. What are some of the industry trends that affect this organization?
7. What are some of the organization's greatest challenges?

Find the company's website using a search engine like Google. Or just call the company and ask for its website address. These are also often listed in business journals, the Yellow Pages and on company brochures and business cards. If you don't have access to the Internet, use a computer at a public library, your state's JobLink Career Center or a college career center.

You can also learn about the organization by asking questions of people who already work there. People in your network may also be able to provide you with names of people within the organization who could talk with you.

Using a Combination of Strategies

A combination of methods is essential for a successful job search; you can't just do one thing anymore. Develop a strategy that works best for the occupation you're seeking. Consult with people in your field or with a career counselor to see what they suggest.

1. If I haven't said it enough already, network! The more people who know you're looking for work, the better your chances of finding work.

2. Use Internet search engines, job board sites, company websites, industry specific websites, blogs and social networking sites.

3. After researching a business, call and ask to speak directly with the hiring manager, inquire about possible openings and ask to set up an appointment.

4. Register with your local JobLink Career Center, state unemployment office or other job placement agency. (Some private agencies may charge a fee.)

5. Attend local and school job fairs.

6. Search job postings in newspapers, professional/trade journals, other publications and online help-wanted services.

7. Watch the business section of your local paper for companies moving into the area, expanding operations, getting patent approvals or awards. These companies are probably hiring.

8. Take a drive through nearby industrial parks, shopping centers and office complexes to find worthy companies you can contact.

The Google Email Trick

I like to use a trick where I find a hiring

manager's name via a LinkedIn search or a general Google search. I choose search terms to describe the department, title and company, using a Boolean search. Once I find the hiring manager's name, I then look for a general company email address. Here's how: As a search term, I use the @ sign followed by the company's website domain name. This shows me the pattern the company uses for personal emails, which might be "firstname.lastname," or some combination of initials and last name. Once I know that, it's easy to insert the hiring manager's name in place of whatever name I found while searching. Now I have an actual email address for the person doing the hiring.

For example: If I were trying to find a human resources manager at Goodrich, I would search LinkedIn for some possible names. If LinkedIn doesn't provide me the contacts I need, I go to Google and type "human resources manager" "Goodrich" "Wilmington, NC." Once I locate a few relevant names in my targeted area —let's say I use an HR manager named Jane Doe—I type "@goodrich.com" or "email @goodrich.com" in Google to find an email. Let's say Jim Smith came up, with "james.smith@goodrich.com." Then I would email jane.doe@goodrich.com and hope it doesn't bounce back. It might take some time to research an accurate email address, and some larger companies might require a middle name or even add some numbers to the person's name, but this technique has worked more than 80 percent of the time in my own personal research.

G

Google Yourself Into Your Next Position

"It is a mistake to look too far ahead. Only one link of the chain of destiny can be handled at a time." — Winston Churchill

This is an effective way to tie in search engines with recruitment strategy. Recruiters use certain tailored search commands that can send back exact information relating to their search, and your resume just might turn up in one of those searches.

In the last chapter, I mentioned a Boolean search. This uses logical commands, such as "and," "or" and "not," to help narrow your search. Some other commands, as you'll see, help find specific terms in the different parts of a web page.

These are some common Google commands. Use this exact format, including spacing and quotation marks. In these examples, we use "HVAC Mechanic." Replace this with your job title or similar terms that pertain to your job search and industry.

Here I list the search command, followed by its result.

[jobs OR employment OR careers OR career] "HVAC Mechanic" [Cleveland or OH or Ohio]

Yields

Job lists for an HVAC mechanic in Cleveland, Ohio

INURL:Resume "HVAC MECHANIC"

Chiller
Yields
HVAC mechanics' (with chiller machine experience) resumes that are in the URL as a title

INTITLE:Resume "HVAC MECHANIC" Chiller
Yields
HVAC mechanics' (with chiller machine experience) resumes that are in a title of a website

INTEXT:HVAC INTEXT:MECHANIC INTEXT:Resume
Yields
Chosen keywords ("HVAC, Mechanic and Resume") in the body of the website

ALLINURL: Resume Mechanic HVAC
Yields
All keywords "Resume, Mechanic and HVAC" in URL of website

ALLINTITLE: Resume Mechanic HVAC
Yields
All keywords "Resume, Mechanic and HVAC" in website title

ALLINTEXT: Resume Mechanic HVAC
Yields
All keywords "Resume, Mechanic and HVAC" in text of website

FILETYPE:PDF Resume
Yields
Resumes with PDF file types

SITE:*Carrier.com* HVAC MECHANIC
Yields
The word HVAC MECHANIC on Carrier's
website

DEFINE: HVAC MECHANIC
Yields
Online dictionaries defining the chosen
word ("HVAC Mechanic")

LINK:*IHACI.ORG*
Yields
Pages linked to the page entered
("*Ihaci.org*")

INFO: *Recruiting.com*
Yields
Information on this link ("*Recruiting.com*")

ID: *Recruiting.com*
Yields
Information on this link (alternative to INFO
search)

~QA
Yields
Synonyms for keywords entered, like
"Quality Assurance" or "questions and answers".
Look for the bold words that come up.

"Resumes AND Mechanic NEAR
Reference*"
Yields
Resumes with the word "Mechanic" near the
word "Reference or References"

Related:*Google.com*
Yields
Competitors of *Google.com*

These are some special commands and symbols that are also very useful in Google searches.

*MECHANIC

The asterisk substitute for an unknown word, so this would display AUTO MECHANIC, HVAC MECHANIC, AIRPLANE MECHANIC

Resume -Submit -Jobs -Openings -Apply

The minus sign omits words after the main keyword, so this finds resumes on pages without the words SUBMIT, JOBS, APPLY and OPENINGS

Resume (Sales | Marketing) "Carrier"

The "pipe" symbol (|) replaces the word "or" in a Boolean search, so this finds resumes of sales or marketing people at Carrier

Resume Mechanic 90606..95112

The two dots are the numbers range shortcut, so this finds mechanics' resumes that have ZIP codes between 90606 and 95112

H

Hidden Job Market

"A friendship founded on business is better than a business founded on friendship." — John D. Rockefeller

For every employer that must downsize, there's an employer that needs to hire the right person for the right job. In any circumstance, businesses are always hiring someone who can make them profitable now!

"We have a hiring freeze" doesn't necessarily mean a company isn't hiring. It means it's not increasing its headcount. Every year most companies have 20 to -25 percent turnover, so in a 1,000-employee company, 200 to 250 people are going to turn over naturally. Those companies are still hiring but they may not tell you so. In fact, 80 percent of jobs are not publicly advertised.

Networking is crucial for finding the hidden job market. Use your current network and these contacts.

Contacts in the Hidden Job Market

1. Companies you have interviewed with in the past. If you were close to getting a job, go back and see if they have any current openings. They'll be glad to re-consider you.

2. Previous managers and co-workers. They already know your worth, making it easier to recommend you to others. If you're still employed, make sure these people will honor your confidentiality.

3. Members of organizations you were

active in: fraternities, sororities, professional business associations, charity groups, fundraisers, athletic clubs, etc. In addition, contact local companies that support these groups through sponsorships or grants. Find the employers, which in turn will lead you to the jobs.

4. Recruiters focused on your industry. Give them referrals to qualified candidates and they will help you in your job search. The nature of their work makes them an invaluable source of information and contacts.

5. Business organizations in your field. Join them. More important, stay involved. Join committees, become a committee leader or get on the Board of Directors. You meet relevant people while creating a brand for yourself by showing your commitment to your industry.

6. Non-profit organizations, especially if you are in the private sector. They value talent from any industry to help with management, marketing, sales and consulting. Target organizations that support your passion or cause. Visit *npo.net*.

7. Government sector: the Peace Corps or local government. They have the ability to provide great benefits.

8. Your own advisory board of mentors. Connect with a few individuals in your industry whom you respect and can contact to guide you through your career.

9. Companies that accept volunteers. They will appreciate your help. Act as you would if you were being interviewed; they are considering you as a future employee.

10. International companies opening locations in your area. Building their staff with local talent saves them money —no relocation expenses.

Applying directly saves them recruiting costs. They also benefit from employees who know about the area and its market.

I

Interviewing

"Success depends upon previous preparation, and without such preparation there is sure to be failure." — Confucius

Interview Training

Plan & Prepare

1. Know your Resume inside and out, line item by line item. Know your cover letter, too. Be prepared to explain each item.

2. Call ahead the day before the interview to confirm your appointment.

3. Know the exact address of where you are going. Get detailed directions on how to get there and how long it takes, including traffic time.

4. Know everything you can about the person you're interviewing with: their name, job title, responsibilities, needs, history with the company, and anything you might have in common with them, like previous workplaces, alma maters, etc.

5. Find out where the employer is in the hiring process

6. Think like a consultant when preparing for an interview, so you can present your true value and worth.

7. Try to think ahead to the interview. If there is a possibility you will be required to perform a task, be prepared. For instance, if you are applying for a job as a welder, you may be asked to demonstrate your skills on the spot. Have your work

clothes and tools available at the interview.

8. Research to be well informed about the job market in general and for the industry in which you're applying.

9. Look up everything you can find on the company's website about the company , its industry and its executives' background. Check out the company on Yahoo Finance. Look up its most recent news, general industry trends and its place within those trends, industry ranking, products, customer base, and basic financial information. A few hours of research prior to an interview is a worthwhile investment in landing a job that can turn into a career! If possible, bring up this information during the interview to impress the hiring managers.

10. Figure out how you can tie your past experiences to the job, particularly in terms of the company's current situation and objectives.

11. Research any challenges facing the company or department so you can discuss how you can help tackle them.

12. Know who your competition is. Use this knowledge to figure out where you fit in and how you can bring value to the company. You need to show how you will outshine and outlast the competition.

13. Anticipate difficult interview questions and prepare possible answers before starting to interview.

14. Make a list of questions to ask during the interview.

15. Know which interviewing skills you possess that make you stand out. Capitalize on these during the interview.

16. Be sure to rehearse, so your comfort level is high.

17. Print extra resumes. Bring them with you, in a professional-looking binder that also holds a pen and a notepad.

18. Try to schedule interviews outside your current work time or in early morning or late afternoon. When you ask the interviewer to schedule an appointment outside the normal time frame, mention that you're very respectful of your current job, and don't wish to upset anybody.

19. Always dress up a level. I you're going to interview as a fast food worker, dress like you're going for the manager's job.

20. Clean up your social networking sites. Potential employers are now going onto Google or a personal networking account—Facebook, Twitter and the like—and using it as a prescreening process. Those spring break party pictures can and will hurt you. A study showed that 50 to 60 percent of employers chose not to hire a candidate after seeing his or her social-network profiles online.

Interview Session

Employers have four main concerns when hiring a new employee:

1. Do you have the skills and experience to do the job?

2. What kind of person are you?

3. Will you fit in at the company and benefit us?

4. What will you cost us?

When asked, "Why do you think you are a fit for this job?" answer with:

1. "I have the potential to benefit the company in two areas." Mention two areas where you are sure you can add value.

2. "I can answer that positively for two reasons." Mention two examples or facts as proof.

3. "My three strongest qualifications for this job are _____, _____ and _____." Always emphasize your skills!

4. "Based on the information you have shared with me today, I can say that I have the potential as well as the enthusiasm and persistence that you expect from someone working for your company." Give examples.

5. "I have encountered situations and challenges in my previous jobs that are similar to those involved with this position and I have a successful track record." Elaborate on one of these examples.

Keep in mind that you are selling yourself to everyone you meet. This means the receptionist, the assistant, people you pass walking in, people in the elevator. If everything goes well, you will be working with these people! The more people you leave with a good impression, the better your chances are of being remembered. Project yourself as someone who is pleasant, thoughtful, helpful, and prepared.

Be ready to demonstrate these qualities. Employers are interested in applicants who:

1. Are goal-directed and have a good sense of what interests them, based on their strengths.

2. Have some knowledge of the organization and why they want to work there.

3. Are confident of their potential to contribute to the organization. Sell your soft skills, too. If you arrive early and leave late, are willing to learn new responsibilities and can wear multiple

hats, explain that to them.

4. Can discuss past experiences that demonstrate the skills and abilities that are important to the employer.

5. Are not late. If possible, arrive 15 or 20 minutes early for the interview. Find a place to gather yourself and check your appearance, make sure your tie and clothes are straight and not wrinkled; get your paperwork in order and your thoughts together. Turn off cell phones and other electronic devices before the interview.

6. Alone. Do not bring anyone with you. If you are sharing a ride with someone, they must wait in the car or find a nearby coffee shop.

7. Initially confident. Introduce yourself with a confident handshake and a smile! First impressions go a long way. Make yours a great one! First impressions are made in the first eight seconds and hiring decisions are made in the first 35 seconds. That is why it's so important to get off on the right foot and build instant rapport with the interviewer. That rapport enhances your ability to connect at a deeper level. You may even create feelings of trust and friendship.

8. Positive. Maintain positive body language. Sit up straight and look interested. Maintain eye contact with your interviewer. If you're being interviewed by more than one person at a time, be sure to maintain eye contact with everybody. Keep your focus and intensity level high throughout the interview.

9. Listeners. Listen closely to your interviewer. Rephrase the question your interviewer asks and use it as the beginning of your answer. This saves you from wasting your interviewer's time, and shows you're a careful listener. Answer

questions specifically, briefly and to the point. Make sure you give all interviewers the information they need to assess whether you're the right fit for the job. Don't ramble on and on. Remember: no one has ever listened themselves out of a job!

10. Not afraid to clarify a question. If you don't understand the interviewer's question, ask for clarification. Don't start rambling to cover up the fact that you didn't understand.

11. Not afraid of asking questions. So ask them! Asking the right questions show you can think strategically, and helps you decide if the position is right for you. If it hasn't come up already, end the interview with this question: "What are you looking for in a candidate to fill this role?" If the answer doesn't match your expectations, then you need to speak up. Keep in mind, the interview is also for you to decide if the job is right for you!

12. Knowledgeable about their resumes. When the interviewer refers to your Resume, focus on your accomplishments, not just your job duties.

13. Confident during the interview itself. Don't be intimidated by interviewers. They don't want you to fail; they want you to show them why you'll succeed with their company. The sooner they hire you, the sooner their—and your—search can end. Don't be intimidated by any questions your interviewer asks. The ability to think on your feet is an important asset, so show your interviewer you can do that. Be confident with your responses!

14. Respectable and can filter themselves. Never curse or swear during an interview, even if the interviewer does. Be the true professional! Don't get too comfortable, either, because it's still an interview. Becoming too casual after you develop a rapport with the interviewer can be a

double-edged sword.

15. Don't bash previous employers. Don't give any negative answers or speak badly about current or past employers, managers or experiences. When an interviewer asks specific questions about your current or past employer and tries to trick you into giving negative answers, don't fall for it! Behavioral questions are designed to make you sweat and turn negative. Be positive and consistent with your responses to all types of questions. Always prepare positive answers beforehand. See the silver lining in everything.

16. Aren't afraid to answer truthfully. When asked, "What are your weaknesses?" answer it by stating where you fit and were you may not fit in the organization as it relates to your skills. It's a good idea to create a list of assets you can draw from during the interview. This should include any anecdotes that may relate to the position you are interviewing for.

17. Are still human. Don't worry about being nervous. It's a natural response. Use that nervous energy to your advantage and be enthusiastic, but be careful not to overstate answers or talk too much.

18. Aren't jumping ahead of themselves. Never ask the company about salary or benefits packages until after you receive a job offer.

19. Aren't too eager. Never try to close too soon. Sometimes employers will drag their feet, so you must remain patient.

20. Aren't eager enough. If you really want this job, don't leave without expressing your genuine interest in getting this job.

21. Enthusiastic. From the time you walk in until the time you return to the parking lot, express

your excitement, smile and greet everyone you encounter. Remember not to stop this until you've in your car and leaving the complex. I once had a candidate who changed clothes in the parking lot. The hiring manager saw this and immediately ruled out that candidate.

22. Add value. Explain to them, "Here's the value I can add to your business; I'm not just looking for a job." Be smart towards that particular employer and have more information and ideas about that particular company. Also add some ideas about how to improve their business and bottom line. It will make you stand out from other people who are interviewing. All in all, it's good to get creative. By showing you can add value to their business, you can add value to the interview itself.

23. Not lacking value. If a candidate says she's worried about laid off from her present job, that's not good, because it shows the interviewer she's not valued at her current position.

24. Aren't worried about confidentiality. If you're interested in remaining confidential throughout the interview process, tell them so. You can mention it briefly by stating, "My current employer doesn't know I'm seeking a more challenging opportunity, so I request your confidentiality during this application or interview period."

Negative Body Language

Avoid these actions, so the interviewer knows you are interested. These actions are also distracting and annoying.

Doing this: Makes the interviewer think you are
Avoiding eye contact: Dishonest, indifferent,

insecure, nervous, passive

Biting lip: Anxious, fearful, nervous

Scratching head: Bewildered, confused

Flaring nostrils: Angry, frustrated

Folding arms: Angry, defensive, disagreeing, disapproving

Narrowing eyes: Angry, offended

Raising eyebrows: Disbelieving, surprised, unprepared

Shifting or slouching in seat: Apprehensive, bored, restless, uncomfortable

Tapping feet: Anxious, nervous

Wringing hands: Anxious, nervous, scared

Question Categories

Interviewers ask a wide range of questions, so be prepared with answers in these question categories.

1. Work and education: What have you done and learned? Why did you leave your last job? What did you like most about your last job? What did you like least about it? What is your management style?

2. Skills and competency: What can you do? Describe a challenging work issue you had to face. How do you handle pressure? What is your most significant career accomplishment?

3. Personality, values and goals: Who are you? What makes you a good team member? Where do you see yourself five years from now? How have you grown in the last few years?

4. Behavioral and situational: Can you tell a story? Tell me about a time when you had to juggle priorities to meet a deadline. If we were to hire you, what would you do in the first 60 days?

5. Job match: Are you a match? Describe your ideal work environment. What aspects of the job will you like least? Why should we hire you for this position? What do you expect your starting salary to be?

Addressing a Layoff

A layoff can be an unpleasant experience and probably not one you want to relive over and over during interviews. The way you handle this topic can make or break an opportunity to move forward with your career and leave the past behind.

Do's

1. DO be the first one to bring up your layoff. Many times a recruiter starts off with, "Tell me about yourself." Tell them about your career achievements and goals first, and then take the opportunity to explain your recent layoff. You can explain it on your own terms, instead of letting the interviewer formulate questions about it. Avoiding or hiding the issue only makes your interviewer think you didn't take the layoff well or that you have more to hide.

2. DO mention if it is related to the recession. Today, even though layoffs can be embarrassing, many recruiters aren't surprised when candidates mention a layoff resulting from the poor

economy.

3. DO mention if you were part of a mass layoff, meaning you were one of many or your whole department was eliminated. A mass layoff takes the attention off why you, personally, were laid off. A single person getting laid off makes a recruiter wonder. A good way to describe a mass layoff is, "There was a staff decrease. Two hundred positions were eliminated, including mine."

4. DO tell them what you have been doing in your time away from work. Be prepared, because they do ask about this. Always tell them job-searching and networking has become your number one priority! Tell them if you took a month to relax. Tell them if you have been doing consulting and freelance work. Be honest.

Do Not's

1. DO NOT make it a complex story. If you are still upset about your layoff, don't let it show, and don't ramble on about why you were let go. Telling a complicated story (there was reorganization, and your boss told you not to worry, but they kept your co-worker instead because she had more experience ...) indicates there was more reasoning behind your layoff. Simply say, "There was a reorganization and unfortunately my position was eliminated." Move on to the next question.

2. DO NOT speak negatively of your last employer, co-workers or the job itself. This is very unprofessional, and again, makes your interviewer think twice about why you were laid off.

3. DO NOT forget that you can say so if you're uncomfortable answering. If your interviewer keeps asking about the layoff, tell them

you prefer not discussing it. This doesn't affect whether you get the job or not.

Phone Interviews

Preparation

1. Have these items ready and in front of you: your Resume, job description, questions to ask the employer, notes about the company, and your calendar or schedule.

2. Ask a career counselor, HR professional, or even a reliable friend to practice a telephone interview with you. Get feedback on your answers, voice inflections and any recurring flaws in your speech: "like," "um," "er," and "uh."

3. Be ready to give examples of your accomplishments and previous work experiences.

4. Sell yourself in every response.

5. Write down the name(s) of your interviewer(s) so you can refer to them by name, and write them a Thank You "thank you" note afterwards.

On the Phone

1. Never conduct a phone interview while driving in your car!

2. Conduct your telephone interview in a quiet place. Don't allow children or pets in the room. Don't answer another phone or the door bell, or permit any other distractions during this time. Turn off any electronic devices that might make noise.

3. Stand up to project your voice better.

4. Be enthusiastic and smile. It comes through in your voice.

5. Speak directly into the telephone, slowly and clearly. Remember, your voice is all the interviewer has to distinguish you from other candidates.

6. Use a land-line telephone, if possible, instead of a cell phone. You'll have a better connection and less chance of being disconnected.

7. Ask for clarification when needed, especially if you're unsure about the question and need time to process your answer.

Phone Etiquette

1. Always sound professional and ready to speak to the hiring manager or recruiter, but be prepared and have a well-memorized or written-out message in case you need to leave a message. This should be a variant of your elevator speech.

2. If you leave a message, always leave your name and number twice. Say your name at the beginning and end of the message. Give your number twice at end of message, repeated back, slowly and distinctly.

3. Leave your message slowly and carefully so the recipient can take notes without having to replay it.

4. Let the recipient choose when to call you back by stating, "Please give me a call at your earliest convenience."

5. If you do speak to someone, always start off with a brief introduction and be sure to ask if it's a good time "Hi, this is Matt Warzel, calling about the sales position advertised in the newspaper. Is this an OK time to speak?"

6. If you do speak to someone, use that time to schedule a meeting in person and not to speak in

further detail, unless they wish to do so.

7. The best time to call is Friday afternoon after 3:30 p.m.

Lunch Interviews

Lunch interviews are becoming an increasingly popular recruiting method. Some interviewers are so busy that meeting you for lunch is the only way to fit you into their schedule. It also allows them to assess your business credentials, while observing your table manners, social skills, and ability to mix business with pleasure. The lunch interview may also be a test if the job you're seeking requires a lot of "working lunches" and meetings, or face-to-face interaction with clients.

As if regular interviews weren't intimidating and stressful enough, now you have to eat lunch while selling yourself! Fear not, I'm going to discuss how you can listen, give intelligent responses and present confidence, all while enjoying a meal.

Selecting the Venue

In the rare instance that the interviewer asks you to choose the dining venue, choose somewhere that's not too expensive and not too casual. You may want to ask what type of food the interviewer likes, then pick a place where you know the service and food is good. Reserve a nice table the day before. Get there early on the day of the interview. Let your host or server know you're there for a job interview and that you need to make a good impression.

Minding Your Manners

No matter how casual the settings, maintain proper table manners. Be mindful of any bad habits and suppress them during a lunch interview.

1. The rules of an office interview still apply, which include dressing properly and not answering your cell phone.

2. Get there a little early so you can settle yourself and make yourself comfortable. You may order water or other acceptable drink, but don't order food until you both are ready to order.

3. When possible, let the interviewer guide seating. If he motions you to choose the seat, then feel free to do so.

4. Be polite, courteous and respectful to everyone, especially your servers. Always say "please," "thank you," "sorry," "excuse me," etc. The interviewer is assessing your personality and behavior to determine if you are a good fit for the company.

5. Be aware of your actions and mannerisms.

6. Sit up straight and comfortably.

7. Don't pick your fingernails.

8. Don't put your elbows on the table.

9. Don't lean on the table.

10. Put your napkin in your lap shortly after taking your seat.

11. Wait until everyone has been served to begin eating.

12. Use the proper utensils.

13. Don't play or make noise with your utensils or other items.

14. Don't cut up your entire meal at once.

15. Cut food into small pieces and eat small

bites.

16. Chew slowly with your mouth closed.

17. Don't talk with your mouth full.

18. Don't make unpleasant remarks about the food, the place or anything else.

19. Don't belch, sneeze, blow your nose, etc.

20. Don't lick food from both sides of your utensil.

21. Don't place unwanted food on the table.

22. If finger food is served, never put your fingers in your mouth or lick them.

23. If you are sharing a dish, as in "Seinfeld," no "double-dipping"!

24. Do not make the sound of eating or slurping.

25. Drink from the right and eat from the left. Think "BMW" to remember the table setting: Bread plate (and fork) on your left, Meal in the middle, and Water glass on your right.

26. The fork goes in your left hand and the knife goes in your right hand. Use the knife and fork to cut your meal, not tear or butcher it.

27. No matter how much you may dislike what you ordered, or if your server somehow messed up your order, just go with the flow. Show that you are sensible and composed.

28. Be prepared. If you feel unsure about your habits and table manners, do some research and consult the experts.

29. To help yourself prepare, dine with a good friend and ask for honest feedback.

30. Refer to the well-known etiquette books by Emily Post.

Ordering

As much as you would like to, even though you are being treated to a nice meal, you can't just order whatever you want. This is still an interview, so you must maintain professionalism and formality throughout the meal.

1. Don't order an alcoholic drink, even if the interviewer does. Order water, juice, iced tea, coffee, lemonade or a soft drink, unless sodas cause you to burp.

2. Order foods that can be cut into small pieces with a knife and fork.

3. Avoid messy or hard-to-eat foods that have to be eaten with your hands. That includes sauces, gravy, soup, spaghetti, wings, etc. Even some salads can be messy—and loud. You don't want to get anything on yourself, or worse, on your interviewer!

4. Avoid foods that have a strong or unpleasant order, such as onions, garlic, etc. Don't be remembered as the "candidate with bad breath".

5. Avoid loud foods—anything crunchy and noisy to eat—so you can have a civil conversation. Restaurants can be noisy as it is, so don't make it harder to hear each other.

6. Avoid foods that require a lot of chewing.

7. Order what the interviewer orders, or something similar and in the same price range. If you're worried about ordering something too expensive, or whether it's OK to order an appetizer, dessert, etc., the best thing to do is follow your interviewer's lead.

8. Order the same number of courses, no matter how hungry you are. Try to finish eating at about the same time as your interviewer. You don't

want to be sitting there while the recruiter is still eating. Likewise, you don't want to be the last one done because you've been talking.

9. If you're asked to order first, order something moderately priced, light and easy to eat; use your common sense.

10. When in doubt, simply ask your interviewer, "What do you recommend?"

Discussing and Dining

It can be tricky to balance food and conversation wisely. In most cases, you should do more talking than eating.

1. Cut and take small bites so you don't delay too much after being asked a question. Small bites are easy to pick up and easy to chew. Also, you don't have worry about getting a stomach ache.

2. Never gesture with your hands while holding your utensils, especially the knife!

3. Don't pick at your food. It makes you look nervous and unconfident.

4. Don't feel like you have to keep talking so you don't eat at all. This can be interpreted as nervousness.

5. Listen and use proper eye contact.

6. Ask questions. When going to any interview, have questions prepared. You learn about the company and show that you care. During a meal, it also gives you a chance to eat while your interviewer responds.

7. This is a great time to ask about the company's culture. Try asking, "Why do you enjoy working for the company?" or "What are characteristics of successful people at the company?"

8. Lunch conversation tends to flow more easily, because it's a more relaxed format. Talk about companies you used to work for, your family, hobbies, and travels. These topics let the interviewer find out a lot more about you. As you become more comfortable talking, be careful not to divulge any information you have intentionally left off your Resume.

Concluding the Meal

As with a typical office interview, let the interviewer set the pace and tone. If there's no hurry after the meal, order a cup of coffee and keep talking. But recognize cues that the interviewer wants to wrap it up, such as asking if you have any final questions or looking around for the server.

1. If the interviewer orders dessert, then feel free to do so. Otherwise, don't order it.

2. The interviewer pays, so don't offer to pay, pitch in, or use coupons or gift certificates. It's not expected, and actually comes off as awkward rather than polite.

3. Don't ask for a doggy bag, no matter how delicious your meal. It's inappropriate.

4. Reiterate your interest in the job and the company.

5. Say "Thank you" with a firm handshake. Thank the interviewer for taking the time to meet with you and that you enjoyed and appreciate the meal.

6. Follow up with a "Thank you" letter the next day, thanking the interviewer again for the nice meal and their time.

Post-Interview

1. You did your best. Now remember to let

it go.

2. Always follow up an interview with a "Thank you" letter within 24 to 48 hours.

3. Understand that the interview is just part of the job search process and there may be many subsequent meetings.

4. Never accept or reject a job until it is offered to you and you have weighed out your options, including all the details of offer package.

5. Maintain relations with the company via email or mail every other month. Even if you didn't get the first job you applied for, they may need you six months or even a year from now.

6. Don't get upset if you don't get the job. Interviewing always gives you good practice and new contacts in the process.

7. Don't badger an employer with phone calls if they have decided to hire another candidate. They get plenty of calls from candidates and it can become irritating to hear repeatedly from someone they can't place into a job at the moment.

Correspondence Tips

1. Start off with, "I hope all is well."

2. Use salutations such as, "Best regards" or "Warm regards."

3. Always include your contact information.

4. Be kind, positive and thankful.

5. Show your relevant interest in the job.

6. Show your appreciation for any correspondence and interviews they provided.

7. Reiterate your skills or any important information you might have not offered while interviewing.

8. Remind them of some key highlights that

occurred during the interview.

9. Update them with important information they might have requested.

10. Convince them why you're the solution to their human capital needs.

J

Joining a Recruiter's Blacklist

"Patience is bitter, but its fruit is sweet." — Jean-Jacques Rousseau

There are reasons why recruiters or hiring managers don't call back some job-seekers: blacklists! In today's tough job market, desperate job-seekers are pursuing what few jobs are available. Hiring managers have plenty of applicants to choose from, so they are justifiably selective and quick to record any negatives they discover.

If you are blacklisted, recruiters won't submit you to jobs today, or even years from now. Even if you're not on an actual "list," recruiters do remember if you left a bad impression. They also pass the word along to fellow recruiters, and they remember bad candidates even if they change companies.

Recruiters have a process called the recruiter's pipeline. You want to get on it. This is a small binder or software manager that recruiters use to store candidates they want to hire down the road. A recruiter is always told to recruit the candidate, not the job. So if we locate a candidate we think is really strong, but don't have an opening that quite matches his qualifications, we'll put this candidate's contact information and Resume into our pipeline. Then we make sure we reach out to him every other month, until that one day where we can finally place him.

Recruiters will also find people who capable to do a job. That means, even if you've never done the job they're seeking someone for, they might consider you if your career path dictates that opening as your next logical step. Most of the time, the ideal candidate is someone who works in the exact same capacity with a competitor, so a new hire can hit the ground running. But even if you don't fit that description, don't sell yourself short. If you're a line supervisor for an auto plant and there's an opening for a production supervisor, you might be considered. The reason is that the new job would be a logical career move if you "worked your way up" with your previous company. Start applying to gigs that are one ring on the ladder above you and you might just land some interviews where you can sell your credentials and ability to learn quickly.

If you're in the pipeline, a recruiter will find a place for you. But if you get yourself blacklisted, all those doors will be closed.

Tips for Avoiding Recruiters' Blacklists

Do's and Don'ts

Recruiters never want to hire any of the 3 L's: liars, losers and loners. Prove that you're none of those by following these tips:

1. DO NOT lie about or exaggerate your experience. Outright lying about experience or skills that you don't have guarantees you a spot on the blacklist.

2. DO NOT pit fellow recruiters against each other. Contrary to what you might think, it doesn't increase your chances of getting a job. You can work with more than one recruiter, but not ones at the same company, unless they are in different office locations, such as MJW Careers Wilmington and MJW Careers Raleigh.

3. DO NOT mass distribute your Resume. Applying for too many jobs with the same recruiter or company makes you look unfocused and creates unnecessary work for them. Make every job application a meaningful one.

4. DO remain courteous and professional, even if your recruiter is not. They are dealing with tons of applicants, so don't take unreturned phone calls or missed interviews personally. Don't attack your recruiter for this behavior; it only leaves a bad impression of you.

5. DO always be interview-ready. Every conversation with a recruiter is an interview, even a casual chat at a networking event. Always be discussing your qualifications. What you may consider harmless joking might rub your recruiter the wrong way.

6. DO clean up your online presence. Recruiters check LinkedIn, Facebook, Google, etc. Even if a comment or photo is old, if it is inappropriate, get rid of it.

7. DO communicate what job you are looking for. Having a good relationship with recruiters doesn't mean you have to accept every job they present. If you aren't interested, say so; it saves everyone time.

8. DO build relationships with recruiters. Always keep your job options open, whether you are employed or not. This means keeping in touch with recruiters at all times.

More Turnoffs

1. Forgetting or missing scheduled interviews
2. Making a faux pas during an interview

3. Handling rejection badly

4. Rejecting an opportunity after a recruiter makes extensive efforts to arrange it for you

5. Taking a counteroffer from another company

6. Demonstrating poor business skills

7. Publicly criticizing other people or companies

8. Failing a background check , which means you can't re-apply for a certain time period

Removing Your Name from a "Do Not Hire" List

Negative notations beside your name can seriously derail your job search. Unfortunately, it's also very hard to discover, much less remove, a bad mark. With so many candidates today, recruiters and hiring managers are even less forgiving. Getting back on their good side requires some extra effort.

Finding Out

1. Speak to key internal contacts and colleagues

2. Ask a reference-checking service to find out if a previous boss made unfair remarks about you

Correcting the Situation

1. Demonstrate your true reliability and professionalism

2. Offer detailed information about candidates for a different job opening and conduct extra reference checks as a courtesy

3. Treat a recruiter to lunch or coffee

4. Request honest feedback about becoming

a stronger candidate next time

     5. Review a background check used to reject you and remove inaccurate records

     6. Consider switching industries or locations

     7. Contact MJW Careers to revise your possibly misleading Resume

K

Keeping Up With Appearances

"Ankles are nearly always neat and good-looking, but knees are nearly always not." —
Dwight D. Eisenhower

Dress for Success

Look your best when you go to a job interview. Dress one step above the dress required for the job. You only get one chance to make a first impression, so make it a good one. Remember, first impressions always count the most!

Before going to the interview, a good step would be to visit the company briefly and see what everyone else is wearing. You must dress appropriately! Do not wear a suit to a construction site. Do not wear a collarless shirt to an executive interview. If you are unsure as to what to wear, it's best to always overdress.

Here are some tips for the big interview day.

Men's Rules

1. Executive/Manager/Entry Level:
A. Black or blue suit with long-sleeved white dress shirt and tie.
B. Shoes that match your suit along with matching belt.
C. Hair is tidy and neat.
2. Individual Contributors:
A. Collared polo shirt with khaki pants.
B. Brown or black dress shoes and

matching belt.

C. Hair is tidy and neat.

Women's Rules

1. Executive/Manager/Entry Level:

A. Dark or tan business suit with solid colored blouse and cream skirt.

B. Shoes that match your suit along with matching belt.

C. Hair is tidy and neat, preferably not seen as a distraction.

2. Individual Contributors:

A. Collared polo shirt with khaki pants or skirt.

B. Brown or black dress shoes and matching belt.

C. Hair is tidy and neat, preferably not seen as a distraction.

L

Letters, Letters and More Letters

"When it is obvious that the goals cannot be reached, don't adjust the goals, adjust the action steps." — Confucius

Cover Letter Preparation

Cover letters are meant to entice the reader to read your Resume. A practical cover letter summarizes your accomplishments and highlights vital elements in your background, as well as persuading the reader to review your Resume. Cover letters are meant to be customized for your job search. They should be based on an interchangeable template so you can easily cater each cover letter towards the exact position for any specific employer. The letter is where you say how you can provide a solution to that particular company's specific needs, making your knowledge appear superior to your competitors.

What are you seeking in this position? Tell them your objective. For example: "I am a 20-year banking expert seeking a financial advisory position with a progressive, leading company in Cleveland, Ohio." Even better, use the company's name.

When preparing a cover letter, a good thing to remember is that it needs to be attention-worthy. Don't say "Dear Hiring Manager," but rather find who will be making the hire and personalize it— target the letter—for them. Don't just state that you need a job in marketing, but rather why you want a job in marketing at this particular company.

Example Cover Letter:

Your Full Name

Street

City, State, 00000-0000

(000) 000-0000

Email Address

April 5, 2014

Recipient's Name
Title
Company Name
Street Address
Suite, unit, floor, etc.
City, State, 00000-0000

Dear [Recipient Name]:

     I am a [job title] with more than 15 years of experience in combined management, finance and sales, and a perfect match for the position of the [name of position] position advertised on the [company portal/newspaper/job board].
     Here is a description of how my experience compares with your requirements.
     Job requirements vs your experience are listed next to each line item by line item. Feel free to take some blubs from your Resume that match up with some blurbs from the job description.
     I understand that with your current business

situation involving the [insert some company knowledge or recent company news or recent industry news; anything relating to the company's current situation], the position might have an opportunity to assist your business during this upcoming [transition, project, merger, acquisition, client engagement].

Insert any experience you might have that directly relates to the company's current situation and you're ability to work within the capacity of the opening.

I would welcome the opportunity to further discuss my skills and this position. If you have questions or would like to schedule an interview, please contact me by phone at (000) 000-0000 or by e-mail at [email address]. I have enclosed my Resume for your review. I look forward to hearing from you.

Warm Regards,

Full Name

Signature

Enclosure: Resume

Follow-up Letter Preparation

Post-interview can be the most crucial time for a job-seeker. While you are still fresh in the hiring manager's mind, you need to act—and quickly! I can provide you with an effective follow-up letter that:

1. Shows the employer your relevant interest in the job

2. Shows your appreciation of the correspondence and interview they provided

3. Reiterates your skills and any important information you might have not provided while interviewing

4. Reminds them about some key highlights that occurred during the interview

5. Updates them with important information they might have requested

6. Tells why you can be the solution to their human capital needs

Example Follow-up Letter:

Your Full Name

Street

City, State, 00000-0000

(000) 000-0000

Email Address

April 5, 2014

Recipient's Name
Title
Company Name
Street Address
Suite, unit, floor, etc.
City, State, Zip Code

Dear [Recipient Name]:

I write to today to thank you warmly for our meeting regarding your open position of [job title] at [company name]. I very much enjoyed our conversation at the [career fair/interview/networking event], and hope that you consider me for the position that you have available.

As a brief overview of my new perspective, our meeting truly enriched my interest and enthusiasm for the open position of [company name] as I learned a great deal about the job requirements, collaboration with other departments, and the room for company growth that you offer. I was particularly impressed with [details about the department and its objectives that you learned about in your first meeting.] I know that my [#] years as a [job title] in this very role give me the same amount of hands-on experience, [specifics of qualities the company is seeking in this position.]

Insert comments about such company-specific details you learned about in the interview, such as core values, relationships between departments, opportunities for promotion, etc. Show that you learned about the company's culture and its needs, and how you would help foster them.

In closing, I thank you again for our meeting and I look forward to hearing from you should you decide to follow up with an interview.

Warm Regards,

Full Name

Signature

M

Maximizing Your Salary

"Famous sides with him who dares." —
Virgil

Overview

Many job-seekers leave the salary verdict up to employers, assuming that they can't negotiate their compensation. While some employers don't encourage negotiation, others are willing to be flexible—for the right candidate!

What to Expect When You're Expecting ... a Raise

First and foremost, get ready to hear "No." When you know it's coming, you can respond unemotionally and state your prepared arguments. Take the initial rejection as a jumping-off point to start negotiation. Reiterate your best arguments and then think about other possible options.

Budget can be a real issue for negotiating a higher salary or raise, especially in a tough economy. Non-cash options are a great alternative if your employer's budget can't grant a raise or higher salary. These perks may seem less attractive than what you hoped for, but they do save you money and make life easier.

If you still come away empty handed, set up another meeting in four to six months or whenever the budget improves. In the meantime, define goals with your boss that you can meet to win a raise the next time.

Reasons to negotiate salary:

1. Your education, experience and skills are worth more than the offered amount

2. The pay range for the position is less than the industry average

3. The area's cost of living is higher and the salary offered doesn't coincide with it.

4. You have received multiple offers with similar salary amounts and benefits

Considerations

You must determine your desired salary range. This gives you more flexibility during negotiation. Most employers already know their range for the position, so you want to aim for the high end.

Consider this issues to determine if your desired salary range is reasonable:

1. Scarcity of the required job skills and experience in market for this position

2. Your career progress and experience

3. Fair market value for the job

4. Level of the job within the organization

5. Salary range for the job within the organization

6. Salary range for the job within the geographic area

7. Salary range for the job within the industry

8. Existing economic conditions within your local job market

9. Existing economic conditions within your industry

10. Company-specific factors such as comparable jobs, culture, pay philosophy, and promotion practices

Research the going market rate for someone with your skills and the type of position for which you are applying. When you know you're making less than your industry peers, you have more ammunition to ask for a higher salary. Check out these and similar websites:

1. *www.Jobnob.com*
2. *www.Salary.com*
3. *www.SalaryExpert.com*
4. *www.SalesHeads.com* (log in and go to Career Resources>Salary Calculator)
5. The Bureau of Labor Statistics at *www.bls.gov/bls/blswage.htm*

To determine your minimum required salary, also take into consideration your expenses, cost of living, saving needs, etc. Once you establish this baseline number, you know the lowest point in your expected (and desired) salary range.

Also, think of a salary range that seems unattainable to you. When you negotiate, fight as if you were fighting for that amount! It causes you to want it more.

Salary Negotiation Techniques in a Declining Economy

To get the money you deserve, you have to ask for it and explain why you deserve it. In a bad economy, wondering "When is the best time to ask for a raise?" is sort of like asking "When is the best time to buy a house?" The answer is, "Whenever you need a house!" So if you believe you need (and deserve) a raise, now is the best time.

Reasons You May Feel Hesitant

1. You feel lucky to even have a job.

2. You worry the boss might view it as "unacceptable" or out of the question.

3. You are afraid of being rejected, demoted, or fired.

4. You feel guilty because friends and colleagues are laid off or cannot find work.

5. In general, fewer Americans are getting a raise, across all industries.

Your boss can't fire you for asking for a raise. Under normal circumstances, it's customary to ask for a raise every twelve to eighteen months. If you received a mediocre raise, ask your boss if you can revisit the discussion in four to six months.

The most opportune time to bring up a raise is after you've earned a major victory for the company or department, or whenever you're on the boss' good side. Schedule a time that's convenient and stress-free for your boss. If you prefer, ask if the boss wants to discuss it over coffee so it feels more comfortable.

Getting Ready

Any time you negotiate salary, you must be confident and be prepared. Compile a list your contributions; for each item, state its impact on the company's bottom line.

Here are some examples:
1. Goals met
2. Projects completed
3. Problems solved
4. Impact on your department or team
5. New ideas or projects generated
6. Tasks fulfilled
7. Knowledge gained
8. Expectations exceeded

9. Kudos from clients and co-workers

In your discussion, follow these guidelines:
1. Acknowledge that you understand the economy and company's financial situation.
2. Do not insinuate that your current salary or job position is a problem.
3. Never give an ultimatum or threaten to quit if you don't get a raise.
4. Don't tell the boss if you have a better offer from another company.
A good tip is to take a picture of your family and put it into your pocket, to remind yourself that this process is all about business. Do not make it personal! Look out for your family and your livelihood.

Increasing Your Perceived Worth

By increasing your perceived worth, you gain a powerful position at the negotiation table. Here are some ways to do this:
1. Present yourself in a positive manner as the "must have" candidate. Employers are more interested in a long-term asset, not just the right person for the job.
A. Make everything flawless: your Resume, interview responses, and dress style.
B. Speak confidently about your accomplishments.
C. Express your goals.
D. Show that you fit in the company's culture.
2. Show that your work value is better than what they realize. Speak in terms of the whole company. Instead of "I can provide good customer

service," explain how "I can retain valued customers and stimulate business activity."

3. Convince the decision-makers that you have more to offer the position and the organization. Establish how your unique skills, experience, and understanding of the company's needs make you more qualified than other candidates.

4. Validate your skills while objectively negotiating the offer. Throughout the actual negotiation period, listen and politely assert the value you've presented.

The Initial Offer and Your Response

When negotiating salary or other benefits, you're also negotiating the foundation of a relationship, so you want to get off on the right foot. You and the employer must come to an agreement that you both feel is fair.

If you're fortunate enough to have multiple job offers, you can sharpen your negotiation skills. Practice with a company you're indifferent about working for. If you're feeling confident, try for the company with the best offer. Remember, if they're negotiating, then you're the leading candidate. Use this power to your advantage.

These are the best steps to take when negotiation begins:

1. Don't negotiate until you have an offer in writing. Let the employer go first with the offer. However, if they ask you first, tell them your salary range, which you determined with the "Considerations" listed above.

2. Restate their offer, and then process it. Make an honest, yet non-emotional, response, based

on your research. When negotiating face to face, be sure your body language doesn't express your emotions.

3. If is the offer is less than you think it should be, indicate that it's lower than your research led you to expect. Be prepared to verify the sources of your research.

4. Counteroffer with your research-based response and desired range. Remain objective, optimistic, and polite.

5. Never accept an offer right then and there. Ask when they need to know your decision. A respectable company doesn't ask you to respond immediately.

Their Response and Your Arguments

Your contact may have to consult with others in the company and get back to you. Rarely do employers withdraw an offer because of a counteroffer, but they may if the company is reorganizing or downsizing. Hopefully the employer returns with a satisfying offer. Otherwise, they state their objection and restate their standing offer.

Numbers always work in salary negotiation, just as they do in your Resume. Never give subjective or emotion-based arguments like, "My co-workers really like me" or "I deserve it." Give undeniable business-related numbers such as, "I increased annual sales by $25,000" or "As vice president, I've reduced my department's employee turnover by 40 percent."

Handling Common Salary and Raise Objections

You may hear some of these objections.

Here are some methods for overcoming them:

Objection: "That's not within our budget for the job." *or* "That's all we have allocated for the job."

Response: Communicate your value to the employer. Persuade them to revise the budget allocation for the position. Point out that the amount is below market value, using your researched range rather than an exact amount.

Show your interest in the job, but mention that you can't justify accepting less than the job's market value.

Objection: "Other employees with similar qualifications and experience aren't paid that much." *or* "You'd be earning more than others in this type of position." *or* "No one else has received a raise, so why do you think you should?"

Response: Persuade them that you should earn more because you're worth more. Give specific examples to support your argument, such as a more advanced degree or more experience than others.

Suggest that they give you a different job title so you fall into a higher salary bracket. Offer to take on additional responsibilities to offset the higher salary. Usually big companies aren't quick to blur job titles and salary levels. But smaller companies that don't use formal pay grades may be more flexible.

Objection: "Your salary history does not justify such an increase." *or* "That's a lot more than your last salary."

Response: Stress that you expect to be compensated for the value of your work and what you plan to achieve within the organization. Help the employer realize you're your previous salaries are unrelated to this job.

Try using these responses in terms of your situation:

"Yes, I earned less at my last job. However, I held that position for three years and the experience I've gained certainly warrants an increase."

"What I'm paid is below market rate. That's one reason I'm looking for a new job. Because of my skills and recent degree, I don't want to accept anything less than market value for a new job."

Objection: "You haven't been working for a while."

Response: Don't let them assume you're willing to work for less, need retraining or are desperate for a job. Let them know that you offer as much as those with current experience.

Stress that your endeavors away from work—training, education, volunteer work, personal projects—enhanced you as an employee.

Accept a lower salary and request a performance review in six months. Ask for a guarantee that if you meet your goals, they will increase your pay to the market value.

Objection: "I'm sorry, but it's our policy not to negotiate."

Response: Look into whether this is true about the company. If it is true, you may have no choice. If it might not be true, say, "I understand you don't normally negotiate salary. But I am an exception, because …"

Negotiate for better non-cash benefits.

Final Offer

Know when to quit. If you sense the employer getting frustrated with your proposals or states that this is all they can do for you, stop and evaluate the existing offer. Don't give the impression that you're impatient or greedy. You may annoy the employer if you push beyond their limits, and they may withdraw offer.

When they come back to you with their final offer, be ready to evaluate it and decide to accept or decline. Once an offer and package is agreed upon orally, always make sure they're going to mail it to you in a signed, written document: an "offer of employment" letter.

Other Negotiables

Salary isn't the only area to negotiate. If the employer rejects your desired salary—or in certain jobs, industries or companies where salary is non-negotiable—you still have options. These other options may be more important to you and might be negotiable.

To better prepare and negotiate, you may want to ask the employer's HR department for information about available benefits and options. These can include:

1. Bonuses based on performance
2. Performance reviews, including the timing and the percentage of pay involved
3. Health, dental, life and disability insurance
4. Retirement or pension plans
5. Vacation and sick days
6. Work-from-home days
7. Tuition reimbursement

8. Overtime policies

9. Profit-sharing plans

10. Stock options

11. Employee discounts

12. Company car and expense accounts, such as commuter expenses

13. Relocation expenses

14. Termination contract

15. Professional association or gym memberships

16. Certifications

17. Childcare

18. Sign-on bonus

N

Networking: Pressing the Flesh

"You can make more friends in two months by becoming interested in other people than you can in two years by trying to get other people interested in you." — Dale Carnegie

Overview

Are you are someone who says, "I HATE networking"? Why? Maybe you feel intimidated, are too shy, lack confidence, or don't know what to say.

In addition to getting someone you know to introduce you to someone you don't know, networking means you do the same for other people. As you network, keep in mind jobs for which other people are looking. You may be able to help some of them get a new job or career. They may return the favor in the future!

Whether you like to or not, networking is a crucial component in career success. I promise, the more networking you do, the easier it becomes! So get out there and start now! The sooner you start, the sooner you are able to do it with ease. Here we offer tips for taking the "work" out of networking.

Networking is Easy! Just Remember, "Own It"!

Objective

Set your objective. Meet (X) number of people in (X) amount of time, per day, week or month, and swap (X) number of business cards.

When/Where

Schedule informal meetings with the person you are networking with and include an agenda of your talking points. Prepare a "script" to make speaking via phone more comfortable.

1. Notify. Tell your contacts about your goals, skills, experience and accomplishments.

2. Inquire. Ask for advice, information and contacts. Don't ask directly for a job!

3. Take away. Obtain at least two more names from each networking connection that you can contact.

Make Networking Work for You

1. Update your Resume and have it ready to distribute. If you don't have them already, get business cards. Sign up for deal alerts on *VistaPrint.com* or one of the many competing online printers, wait for Vista Print or a competitor to offer a free business card deal, and order them!

2. Be clear about whom you are and what you want.

A. If you're wishy-washy when people ask what kind of job you're looking for, it only makes it harder for them to help you.

B. Never respond with, "I'll do any job!" It makes you look not just desperate, but also unsure about your career.

C. If your job preferences vary between industries, that's OK.

D. Determine if there's anything you're willing to compromise on; perhaps relocation?

3. Make sure your online marketing tools

such as Facebook or Twitter are cleaned up and employer-ready. You don't want a potential employer to see something on your social networking sites that might land you in trouble.

4. First, tell the people closest in your life that you need a job. This helps you gain the confidence to approach others later. Inform parents, siblings, parents' friends, professors, career services at your college, past colleagues and bosses. Set up face-to-face meetings to show that you're taking your networking seriously. This also helps each of your contacts to remember to mention you when they encounter a prospective employer.

Work Networking Events

1. Get the most out of networking events.

A. Join industry networking functions by checking online with relevant associations.

B. Research who is attending and make a list of the best people for you to meet.

C. Develop and strengthen relationships by following up with your top connections.

D. Arrange your own networking functions!

2. Look and act appropriately.

A. Practice and know your elevator speech. Use it as your introduction.

B. Be positive, friendly, and enthusiastic. No one wants to talk to (or hire) a bore.

C. Ask questions and listen.

D. Get to know the person and the company.

3. Remember people's names.

A. Use each person's name at least three times during your conversation.

B. Swap cards and write a note or description on the back to remind you who each person is.

C. Later you can forward articles or other information about their industry—or hobbies—to your new connections. This keeps you connected.

4. Getting into a networking group at an event.

A. Stand by and observe the participants' body language until you get an opening.

B. Offer them some refreshments.

5. Getting out of a networking group at an event.

A. Always act interested, even if you're not.

B. Say, "Thank you! I enjoyed talking with you. Enjoy the rest of the evening."

C. Swap business cards and say, "Can I call you so we can discuss this further?"

D. Always close with a handshake and a smile.

Don't forget about unconventional networking places like community events, prayer groups, PTA meetings, charities, political campaigns, local shopping, etc. You never know where your next lead will come from, so keep resumes in your car and business cards in your pocket or purse.

Tips of the Icebreaker

In your first networking conversation with someone new:

1. Always begin with, "Hi! I'm ____. How are you?" and shake hands firmly.

2. Say your elevator speech.

3. Focus on the other person, not yourself.

4. Compliment your new contact.

5. After you have talked business, ask about casual topics like family and spare time.

6. Use whatever lingo and networking tricks you may overhear, if you see them getting a positive response.

Try using these statements as icebreakers or to spark further conversation:

1. "I'd like to know more about [the company, positions available, something else you have researched]."

2. "What an outstanding [booth, event, turnout]!"

3. "Isn't this is a clever [brochure, marketing item]?"

4. "Where do you work?"

5. "What kind of work do you do?"

6. "How did you get into this industry?"

7. "What do you enjoy most about this industry?"

8. "How did you go about getting your job?"

9. "What do you enjoy most about your job?"

10. "What keeps you motivated?"

11. "How are you going to continue growing your business?"

12. "Who is your most challenging competitor? Why is that?"

13. "What is your greatest challenge?"

14. "Which industry websites or blogs do you follow?"

15. "Are you attending other [career fairs, events, conferences] soon? I'm interested in going, too."

16. "If you weren't in your current career, what would you be doing?"

17. "When you're not at work, what do you do for fun?"

Networking Online

Always be networking! Network online and search for networks you're familiar with, depending on your profession.

Final Tips

Join groups on Facebook, Yahoo Groups and LinkedIn and go to *Meetup.com*, *Eventful.com*, and *EventBrite.com* to find groups related to your profession and network with those people. Tweet about the networking events on Twitter to get the word out there for others!

Networking in the virtual world is a wonderful, quick way to make connections, but be aware of how your profile looks online. Employers will search your name and try to dig up information about you online. Stay away from posting party pictures of yourself.

A good tip is to buy someone lunch, because then they'll feel obligated to help you out. Once, an actor bought me lunch because he wanted to dig in and find out more about me and the acting business. To this day, I still respond to every message he sends.

You can always tell how well you're doing at a networking event based on how many business cards you have lying around at home.

Keep up to date with past contacts. In case a

contact is no longer with the company, you can find out who replaced your contact. That lets you continue to build a relationship with that company.

Listen, listen, listen. I hate when people watch me talk to them, and after listening for ten seconds, engage in another conversation! PAY ATTENTION TO ME IF I'M TALKING! If by chance I do that because I might be distracted by a third party interrupting, I always come back and say "Sorry, so you were saying that you think ____." Not listening is worse than not talking!

Join professional & networking associations or organizations such as the Lion's Club, SHRM, BBB, Knights of Columbus or the Chamber of Commerce. Research your position or industry. You'll find some niche groups that will benefit you by hosting networking events.

O

Online

"The production of too many useful things results in too many useless people." — Karl Marx

Knowing where to find a job is the first step. In today's career search, the Internet is vital. Gone are the days that you could rely on faxing and door-to-door marketing. But don't totally discount those methods! Email and the Internet are here and won't be going anywhere, anytime soon. If you need to use a friend's computer or the local library, so be it. Free courses or seminars are always being offered at local colleges or libraries to assist you with accessing and navigating the Internet. Your competition is doing this, so make sure you are, as well.

Most large companies use an applicant tracking system and tailor their searches to Internet job boards. Similarly, most recruiters find potential candidates by searching on the Internet, using keywords found on a Resume. Most companies and recruiters want you to email them a Resume, so setting up a free email account is essential if you don't already have email access. Unless a hiring manager networks his or her way directly to you, you're going to have to learn to use the Internet as a main source to find that right career for you.

This chapter covers crucial Internet job search information, such as: Internet Resume posting, Internet job search, Internet research and Internet marketing. We also include an online search guide that can broaden your search results. This is an exact replica of what recruiters use to search for candidates.

Getting Started

If you don't have Internet access, use a friend or family member's computer or go to your local public library. If you're an Internet novice, enroll in a class to learn the basics of Internet terminology and navigation. Look for free or affordable Internet classes at your local public library, community college, high school, or other institutions that offer these classes to the public. Don't be intimidated or embarrassed. As stated said earlier, in today's career search, the Internet is vital.

Create an electronic version of your Resume with a word processing program, such as Microsoft Word. You may also want to create an Adobe PDF version of your Resume. Depending on where you post your Resume or where you email it, employers may want either a Word version or PDF version.

Set up an email account so you can instantly provide your Resume to employers, networking contacts or recruiting professionals. Free email accounts are available through Yahoo, Google (Gmail) and Hotmail. Create an appropriate and professional email account name, ideally based on your name. Don't use such names as "BeerDrinker@___.com." When you submit your Resume, don't attach a file with a confusing name like "821080res.doc." Instead, use your name or a descriptive label such as the name of the job you're applying for. For instance, "JohnDoeResume.doc" or "MarketingManager.pdf."

Marketing Yourself on the Internet

Here is a list of ways to market yourself on the Internet. I discuss each topic in more detail throughout this chapter.

1. Set up profiles on company portals and job boards to showcase your Resume and skills.

2. Create a personal Resume website tailored towards your skills and Resume. Some can be expensive, but the chances of being found are growing as recruiters are using the Internet as a main search tool. Post a portfolio of projects you've worked on to show skills you can offer to a prospective employer. A link to your website is a natural extension of your Resume.

3. Post your availability as a job-seeker and a brief summary of your qualifications to free classified-based websites including Craigslist, MySpace and Backpage.

4. Join social networking sites including LinkedIn and Facebook. Set up profiles and blogs on those sites and post your Resume and credentials. Use these to divulge industry knowledge, share activities you're engaged in, provide your own networking tips or advice on advancing in a given career.

5. Start a blog on well-known sites such as Twitter, Blogger, TypePad or WordPress to share your professional knowledge and get information from other bloggers. This lets you be proactive and forward-thinking and draws people to you.

6. Join discussion groups on social networking sites such as LinkedIn, Facebook, Myspace, Yahoo Groups and Google Groups to create an Internet presence that you can use to market yourself. Discussion and networking groups exist for different industries, companies, interests, etc.

7. Make connections—building your network—on these networking sites. Get advice and

give advice. Search company names, co-workers, etc. to see whom you have connections with.

8. Promote with advertisements in media.

Internet Resume Posting

Post your Resume on numerous job boards, both general and niche. Activate alerts on those sites, so when a company posts a position that matches your background those alerts are sent directly to your email.

Company portals: Almost all companies post their job openings on their company portal or website. So search all the portals of the main players in your industry and also the larger companies that hire people in your profession. Click on each company's "career" section. Create an online profile and post your Resume so the company's hiring manager or recruiter can find your Resume information. Also, set up an alert before you log off the company's portal.

General job boards: Post your Resume on CareerBuilder, Monster and HotJobs because those sites are where recruiters typically search for resumes first. And why not? More job-seekers use those sites than anywhere else in the world.

Niche job boards within your industry: Perform an online search with your industry's name plus "job board" and review the results. Post your Resume on the sites that turn up and set up alerts.

Association websites within your industry: Most professional associations are easy to find online. By checking out an association's website, you might find a job board or place to post a Resume. Even if not, you may learn about industry events or networking groups. You may also find an opportunity to create an online profile and join a chat board, helping you to stay in the loop with the organization.

Resume distribution services: send out your Resume to thousands of recruiters and direct hiring companies by using:

1. *BlastMyResume.com*
2. *ResumeBooster.com*
3. *ResumeBlaster.com*
4. *ResumeZapper.com*

Keywords

Placing keywords—sometimes called buzzwords—that pertain to your specific skill set, profession, and industry in your Resume helps recruiters find it online. Typing a keyword in a searchable index can bring up any Resume that includes that word. The chances of your Resume being spotted on Google or Monster, for example, are tremendously enhanced among all the clutter of cyberspace. Make sure you add a section at the end of your online Resume that contains a list of the buzzwords relating to your industry. Make sure you use all the various spellings of such words or phrases. For example: HVAC, H.V.A.C., HVAC/R, HVACR.

Personal Resume Website and Blog

You may also consider creating your own website to showcase your skills, your Resume, and examples of your work. When sending out emails, include a link to your personal marketing website. This makes you stand out from everyone else as someone who's serious about your job search!

A personal website is one of the best ways to promote and let the world read all about the benefits of your career brand. Your portfolio should include all your important brand artifacts: Resume(s), mission statement, detailed list of accomplishments, samples of your work, any articles and working papers you've written, transcripts of speeches, awards and honors, testimonials, and more.

Even better, publish content-rich articles, and other keyword-rich materials. These help build your professional reputation as an expert in your field, and lead prospective employers looking for someone with your qualifications directly to your site.

If you're a decent writer and can commit to writing regularly, creating a professional blog is a great tool for building your career brand. A blog is a specialized website that focuses on a particular subject—person, industry, profession—that can include news, analysis, commentary, and links in a variety of formats. These can include print, audio, images, and video. Your blog showcases your expertise and knowledge of your industry or profession. It's an excellent way to build your career brand. An important caution: in your professional blog, or anywhere a hiring manager might see, never mention anything about sex, religion or politics. This chapter talks more about blogs, including Twitter, later on.

Setting Up Your Website in 5 Easy Steps

1. Create an account at one of the low-cost website hosting services. The best known is *www.godaddy.com*. Many other sites offer the same services at comparable rates. So if you prefer, you can follow similar steps elsewhere.

2. Find an available domain for you site by

using the domain search tool. I suggest using some simple variation on your name as your domain. Try to stick with a ".com" or ".net" extension if possible. For example, *"JohnDoe.com"* or *"JohnDoe2014.net."* Once you've established an exclusive domain, click Add and Proceed to Checkout.

3. When you've completed the approval and payment steps, go back to the Go Daddy homepage—make sure you're still logged in—and select Website Tonight under "My Products." If you can't see the Website Tonight button, click Show All of My Products. It will be listed there.

4. In the Website Tonight section, click Use Credit in the yellow box. On the right side, select your domain name and click Continue. The site guides you through the remainder of the process.

5. Once you've established your Website Tonight domain, go back into the Website Tonight section. Check the box next to your domain and click Launch. You'll be guided through a step-by-step process to set up your website.

Internet Job Search

The main advantages of using the Internet as job search tool are that it's accessible 24 hours a day; you can apply to any location, and you're in control of the most detailed possible job search.

The following "Apps" section was written by Josh Weiss-Roessler of *www.weissroessler.com* and is used by permission.

Searching for jobs is stressful. You're constantly putting yourself out there and facing potential rejection (or worse, silence,) racing to make sure you reply to posts fast enough, and looking under every metaphorical rock you come upon hoping to discover that perfect position.

Welcome to the age of applications. "Did you see that app?" is an increasingly common theme running from the executives to entrepreneurs. Luckily, the digital age has brought with it some bonuses for job-seekers that make the search just a little bit easier on you: job-hunting apps. This kind of software runs the gamut, aiding with job searches, retrieving information and files, networking, and organizing.

Here are some of the best apps out there to make your job-hunt less stressful.

LunchMeet: When all you do all day is sift through job postings and send out your Resume, life can get pretty lonely. Not to mention the fact that it can be difficult to land a position if you don't have some kind of contact or "in" at the company. That's where LunchMeet comes in.

After you connect it to your LinkedIn account, it looks for contacts in your industry who have said they are open to networking so you can try to set up a lunch or grab coffee to talk about career opportunities. You can even specify a time and place and then have the program look for people willing to meet up nearby using geo-targeting.

LinkUp: At first glance, this free app for iPhone, iPad and Android just seems like yet another program that lets you search for jobs while you're out and about. The difference, however, is that unlike other apps, it doesn't just search a job board with postings that have been directly submitted. Instead, it looks for jobs on more than 22,000 individual company sites, sifting for the category you choose.

Career Igniter: There's no use finding that perfect job unless you have a Resume ready. One of the best ways to make that look great in a flash is to use a free online Resume builder like the one at Career Igniter. With dropdown menus for each section and prompts to include details like employer information and start and end dates, you'll never forget to include any needed information. Even better, the system will automatically output your Resume to several different templates, letting you see what it looks like so you can choose your favorite.

BusyBee: If you're a freelancer like me, you know how important it is to continually be looking for new clients and jobs. BusyBee assists in this search by allowing professionals in education, construction, engineering, data entry and administration, design, writing, and more to look for work by category. It also sorts by location if you'd like to find jobs close to home. And even people without freelance experience may want to try the app to make extra money or build up their portfolio.

Jibber Jobber: Job searches can quickly become confusing, especially if you're the type of person who likes to apply to lots of places in the hopes that something will pan out somewhere. Jibber Jobber is a great way to stay organized so you don't mistake one company or contact for another and embarrass yourself with a costly mistake.

SparkHire: What if you're trying to find a new job to replace your current one? Chances are, you don't have a whole lot of time to take off for things like interviews, but with SparkHire you don't have to. The site is a job board where you can upload video resumes, as well as interview via recorded video. Employers create text questions for interviewees, who can record video answers and send them in. No more sneaking away for long "lunches" or calling in sick. Those with iPhones can also download the mobile app of the video interview software.

Interview Pro: But before you record those SparkHire videos, you may want to practice with Interview Pro. With more than 80 typical job interview questions, you'll be well-prepared for whatever might come your way. Even better, the program also offers explanations for the questions as well as suggested answers.

Google everything: No, that's not a new piece of Google software but it might as well be. With Google Drive, Docs, Calendar, Alerts, and more, you'll be ready for anything. You can save your Resume on the cloud, share it with employers, collaborate with friends to update it, create reminders for interviews and such on Calendar, and set up Alerts for specific kinds of job postings.

Put the power of these apps in your hands and, who knows, your job search may even end up being something you enjoy.

Essentials

1. Bookmark all the good job board sites so you're constantly checking for the newest job postings that might not come through in an alert. Some postings may have a different job title tailored towards a company that might not use universal job titles.

2. Set up alerts on company portals and both niche and general job boards. Once a position opens up with your title, you receive an email instantly. You can have an edge on competitors by applying

the same day the job was posted and before the next 2,000 resumes come through. Also, set up Google and Yahoo News alerts for your specific job title and industry as well as for general job-hunting techniques. Use relevant keywords such as "job-hunting tips," "mechanical engineer" and "automotive."

3. Search company portals, niche and general job boards, blogs and chat rooms relating to your industry to find employment opportunities.

4. Upload your Resume onto the company's job portal. A company portal is that little link on a website that says "careers." It's the place where, once you upload your Resume, it kicks it to the company's HR staff and allows them to search your Resume on their applicant tracking system. It's important to set up a profile on the company's portal. Make sure you do this for all companies you're interested in. Not only for all companies in your industry, but also do this for large companies and local employers. A mechanic opening at Dell? It might just happen.

5. Instead of going to the major job boards such as CareerBuilder or Monster, start by using Indeed.com or SimplyHired.com. These are job board aggregators. They search jobs on all the other job boards, including company websites. Also use Craigslist, which is a great place to find local job postings in your area.

6. Use indexers and search engines to begin locating resources specific to your occupation and field. Use these sites to locate specific organizations and companies to contact and to look for even smaller, more exclusive collections of job listings.

7. Use general search terms such as "job," "opening," "blog," and terms specific to your

industry, to locate hidden or deeper-result sites. These might have industry experts who speak about everything from new equipment to who's hiring. Try multiple combinations of words used in your industry until you find all information you can digest. Learn the labor market trends on who's laying off and who's hiring. Know your industry!

Internet Research

1. Research your industry and get to know everything about the power players. Learn about labor market trends, which can help you find out who's hiring and what skill sets will be needed in the future. Get used to running long search commands until you find exactly what you're looking for. The search engine is a great tool for anyone.

2. Find salary reports to learn how to gain an advantage during salary negotiations. You can also find salary information on Salary.com.

3. Search employer databases for more information on your industry's power players. Some of these databases are: *Hoovers.com*, *Bizweb.com*, EDGAR Database of Corporate Information, *BBB.org*, *BigBook.com*, *Vault.com* and *DNB.com*.

4. Subscribe to mailing lists or "listservs" hosted by industry experts for up-to-date information on your industry's trends and nuances.

5. Research what titles companies are using. Each company may not only change titles, but some have their own version of a job title.

6. You can tailor your research to local companies to find out local industry trends or cost of living before pursuing employment with a certain company.

7. Search news groups to find the most

recent information on a company or industry.

8. Examine companies' credibility through news reports, review sites and the like.

9. Go to a stock website, like Dow Jones Industrial or Sharebuilder, and check a company's stock. Then look into the message boards about that company's stock to see what buyers, sellers and brokers are saying. Some of those boards' users may be employers who are willing to sign on as "anonymous" and divulge information about the company's leadership team, management practices or business outlook.

10. Network any way you can with industry experts!

Email Etiquette

1. Keep your emails as short and to the point as possible.

2. Use HTML coding—the language websites are built with—to take advantage of tracking, but keep it simple.

3. Intrigue your reader with the email message and get them to find out more by clicking on a link to your Resume website.

4. Spend most of the time on the top three inches of the email, because it's what people see if they're using "preview" in Microsoft Outlook.

5. Ask recipients to forward your email to other people who may be looking for your skills.

6. Use an effective subject line. It must reflect the email's contents, but you also want to make it stand out.

7. Don't send it if it looks like spam: that is, if it's something you would delete without reading.

8. Always use both first and last names in the "from" line. Most people assume email from a

first name only is spam.

9. Don't include attachments in unsolicited emails. Smart email users don't open attachments from someone they don't know, for fear of viruses. But if a hiring manager or recruiter asks you to send them your Resume, then go ahead and do so as an attachment.

10 Correspondence Tips:

A. Begin with "I hope all is well" and include your contact information along with being kind and positive

B. End with "Salutations," "Best Regards," or "Warm Regards."

Webcasts

The following is a list of online webcasts provided by third-party companies that are proven experts in human capital management. Check into appropriate listings that suit your job-hunting needs.

1. *www.astd.org/Digital-Resources/Webcasts/TD*, training and development.

2. *www.careerbuilder.com/jobposter/events/webinar*, job-hunting information.

3. *www.navexglobal.com/resources/131/types/webinars,* training and development.

4. *www.ere.net/webinars,* recruiting.

5. *www.humancapitalinstitute.net,* human resources.

6. *www.peoplefluent.com/resource-center,* talent management.

Job Links

For a list of job links, please refer to Appendix A. There you will find some websites to get you moving on your job searching and posting duties.

P

Pitfalls and Places You Should Avoid Working

"Distrust and caution are the parents of security." — Benjamin Franklin

Steer Clear of These on Your Job Search

At times, job-seekers don't think long enough before they jump into an opportunity, which can backfire and hurt them emotionally and financially. Even if you're feeling desperate in your job search, don't let people take advantage of you and ruin your life! These are some of the jobs out there that aren't worth pursuing.

1. Unpaid internships with small companies that have no brand. Unless they are partnered with colleges and can offer academic credit, avoid unpaid internships. Remember when Kramer in Seinfeld had an intern at his company "Kramerica"? Our point exactly.

2. Buzz marketing companies. These places constantly need agents, who end up being gullible consumers, to receive samples and coupons to give their friends. If people sign up through the website, they don't get money or anything of value, just free stuff to give to other people.

3. Promotional marketing companies. The employers give out sample coupons door to door and earn a profit off consumers buying these coupons for events like baseball games. Sadly, the coupons aren't affiliated with the event sponsor and, therefore, don't work. Avoid being a scam artist without knowing you are one.

4. Any jobs that offer commission for recruiting others, rather than for selling goods or services.

5. Work-at-home scams, like online ads that say "Make $10K a month working part-time from home!" Stay away from anything that sounds too good to be true, because it probably is.

6. Companies that make you pay application fees. No legitimate companies charge you to work for them, so don't assume this is a normal practice. Don't pay an upfront fee for formation about employment or franchises without thoroughly investigating the organization first.

7. Mystery shopping scams. Some may ask you to handle money on your own by using fake checks from the company in place of your own cash, but only after you've spent your own cash. You can find legit mystery shopping companies on the Mystery Shopping Providers Association list.

8. Companies asking for your birth date, Social Security number, credit card information, personal PIN numbers or other personal information via email, online or over the phone. Real employers or business operators don't ask for this information in these ways.

9. Jobs that ask you to pay for training at companies that aren't certified. It's one thing to enroll at a community college for a trade certification or rapid learning course, but it's another to communicate with an educational class only via email and send in money for training and learning materials. Research schools to see if they are a qualified online training institute, such as the University of Phoenix Online.

Basically, if the job is easy or sounds too good to be true, it probably isn't going to pay off.

You need to work hard to garner success.

Online Resources to Detect Fraudulent Businesses

If you're unsure about a company's practices, do some online research and see if any search results yield the word "scam" or "fraud" in the text. Check out business on these sites:

1. The Better Business Bureau at BBB.org
2. Google, Yahoo and Bing
3. Your state's secretary of state office. For example, North Carolina's is *www.secretary.state.nc.us/Corporations*

To report employment fraud, contact any of the following offices:

1. Federal Trade Commission at 1-877-FTC-HELP
2. National Fraud Information Center at 1-800-876-7060 and *www.fraud.org*
3. Your state attorney general's office; for example, North Carolina's at 1-877-5-NO-SCAM and *www.ncdoj.com/consumerprotection/cp_about.jsp*

For more information on employment fraud, visit *www.rileyguide.com/scams.html*.

Q

Questions to Ask at the Interview

"Judge a man by his questions rather than his answers." — Voltaire

Overview

It's essential to ask questions at the end of an interview. Too often candidates will stare blankly for a brief second when asked "Do you have any questions for me?" and follow up with a comment and head shake that insinuates a 'No' response. This isn't good practice. You need to ask a few questions, even if they aren't necessarily your concern at that particular moment. I don't mean asking questions about benefits or pay, but things pertaining to the company's culture, industry trends, business projects, etc. Take a look at some sample questions below.

Sample Closing Questions to Ask

1. "Is there any other information you need from me regarding my application?"
2. "Do you have any hesitations about me for this position?"
3. "How do I compare to my competition?"
4. "Is there any reason why I wouldn't be an asset in the job I'm interviewing for?"
5. "I want to work for your company; can you see any reason how I might not fit into your corporate culture?"
6. "Is there anything hindering me from moving forward in the interview process?"

7. "Is there room for growth within the organization and this department? If so, what's a typical path for an employee in the position I'm being considered for?"

8. "Do you know when I might hear from you regarding the next step?"

9. "Is this a new position? If not, what happened to the previous employee?"

10. "How would you describe the position's responsibilities?"

11. "How would you describe a typical week or day in this position?"

12. "What do you enjoy most about working here?"

13. "What do you enjoy least about working here and what changes would you like to see made?"

14. "Where do I go from here? Can you tell me about the rest of the interviewing process?"

15. "Is there any reason why we can't set up the next interview now?"

Sample Closing Questions Not to Ask

As I've said elsewhere, you should have done your research prior to entering the interview room. Find out as much as you can about the company, its projects, its industry, its leadership and, most important, why it's hiring for the job you're being considered for. Here is a list of questions you you should have answered for yourself before beginning the interview—and to avoid asking at the end.

1. "What does your company do?" Research this information, please.

2. "What's the timeline for raises?" or "What's the vacation schedule like?" Don't target

extended benefits during the interview. You need to be patient with this question, unless you absolutely must know because you have pending offers elsewhere.

3. "Is the job flexible as far as when to start work and end work for the day?" Don't come off as worried about time or being lazy. You want the interviewer to think you're concerned about the job itself, not the time spent on the job.

4. "Does the job require working overtime or weekends?" Wait to find out, because when you're a new employee, sometimes you need to make sacrifices.

5. "How did I do during this interview?" Don't call out the interviewer; it's bad business practice.

R

Resume

"What we learn only through the ears makes less impression upon our minds than what is presented to the trustworthy eye." — Horace

Overview

As a former human resources recruiter with more than ten years of experience, I would commonly go through hundreds of resumes for any particular position. And while it became tedious to sift through the same inadequate pieces of paper over and over, I would always find a diamond in the rough. Remember, the three-second rule is very much alive and breathing. As a recruiter, I go through hundreds, even thousands, of resumes. That means a recruiter's brief three-second glance will dictate whether the rest of the Resume will be read. So you must stand out!

A Resume that stands out can create a sense of urgency, leading a recruiter to present it to the hiring manager without even calling the candidate first. Of course, that isn't the reality, because we do have to pause and track down the "Purple Squirrel." That is the hard-to-find candidate. Recruiters investigate all candidates to see if they really do match up with the opening.

Now you're asking, "What did that person have on his or her Resume to make them stand out?" Simple. They can do the job and the Resume reflects that. As much as I'd like to just spend time on top candidates, I still want to help the rest of the fold, should they ask why they didn't get chosen.

With that, I give you five surefire Resume killers that can become deal breakers, in no particular order.

Get rid of the fluff. People tend to use too many adjectives, such as "fast learner" or "hard working," when describing themselves or their experience. Don't be one of those people! Anyone can claim to be a "team player." These descriptions are subjective and can't be proven. We also don't need to know how you helped Bill get to work for a week when his van broke down. Everyone is a "hard worker" during an interview and even on his or her poorly written Resume. Anyone can use any of these adjectives that aren't verifiable and aren't objective.

It isn't a novel. You don't need to write a paragraph for each job description. I once had a candidate send me a summary of his work experience, as opposed to a nicely formatted section that listed employment dates, employer, location and title. My hiring manager told me it had to be cleaned up before he would even review it. So I passed the memo along to the candidate, who apparently was too lazy, or offended, to make any edits. Even though he would have been a fit for our opening, it was on to the next candidate!

Lack of depth. Write tangible descriptions relating to your skills and duties. Quantify your accomplishments with specific numbers or results you produced. Anything is better than broad generalities. They're annoying and a major turn-off for HR people and managers. Data and numbers showcasing your ability to impact the bottom line is what they want to see. So calculates how you increased revenue or reduced spending for your previous employers and show that on your Resume.

Companies want you to tell them what you can do for them. Your Resume should be quantitative, not qualitative, because numbers make a stronger statement than a list of duties. Remember, employers will know what you can do from your Resume. But you want to make sure you demonstrate your ability execute those duties at a high level. The Resume should show results. If you saved your employer money or time, say so!

One title, one Resume. Tailor your resume to the job you're attempting to land. Market yourself specifically for that job. Hiring managers are focused on what they need and expect your resume to be geared toward that need. If you're interested in multiple job titles, create multiple versions of your resume. Make sure each is based on the company's job description for the title you're applying for. Be alert to each job posting's details, because employers want people who can pay attention to detail. Note that sometimes companies use different titles for the exact same positions. You need to do your research to find out what range of titles you fit into. A company might not be looking for a machinist's mate—a military term—but will hire you as an HVAC mechanic, the civilian term. Employers sometimes don't know your title and sometimes will have to get to the interview to find out what you actually do with that unknown title. And we know that landing the interview is first priority. Thus, change your title from "Machinist Mate" to "HVAC Mechanic" if that describes the work you did.

Out with the old. Objectives are increasingly being replaced by summaries. Companies care more about what you can do for them than about your objective. We all know you're looking for a job, so put a nice small paragraph at the top of the resume to emphasize your skills and abilities. Plus, your summary is half your cover letter!

Not enough keywords. Use words from the job posting to customize your resume each time you send it out. If the job posting says "project management," use that same term resume as it relates to your experience. Most recruiters aren't experts on every single facet of every single opening, so they constantly are seeking information from actual candidates to learn more about the jobs they're trying to fill. Try to help them out and put relevant buzzwords in your resume to help them see you actually have the skills that job posting requires. Most of the time recruiters use those same buzzwords when searching databases to find your resumes. It's always helpful to talk about to customers or clients to learn more buzzwords that you can use on your resume.

Gaps. If you've fallen into the category of a serial contractor or run into repeated lay-offs, it's sometimes a good idea to show the hiring manager your reason for leaving each position. A simple "Laid off" or "Contract expired" blurb right next to the company's name on the resume might help you avoid being tossed out without a chance to defend yourself.

Another tip is that recruiters want to see how much work you can bring in from your prior client contacts, without jeopardizing any non-compete clause from a previous job.

A superior resume displays your marketable or transferable skills and experience. It "pre-sells" you. It's more than just getting an interview; when you walk in, the interviewer's reaction should be: "I've read your resume, and I'm really looking forward to meeting with you." A superior resume puts you ahead of the ever-increasing competition, so you can be confident that you get noticed over the hundreds of other people applying.

Feel free to search other job-seekers' resumes on Google and pull some of their descriptions for yourself. You don't want to copy and paste, but rather use your findings as a template and idea generator. Also, take information directly from postings on job boards. Employers are asking for people to do certain duties; if you can do those things, say so on your resume, using language similar to the posting. Always go beyond that, but it's a starting point to get your brain working in resume writing mode.

Develop a set of questions that a resume needs to answer. Think of it as a list of the resume's necessary elements. As a recruiter, I'm always asking myself while reviewing a resume:

1. When did this person work?
2. Where did she work?
3. What did he do at this job?
4. What was her job title?
5. What was his reason for leaving?

So when you develop your resume, be sure you're saving the reviewer's time by answering all these questions.

Also, check your grammar and spelling. Look for some of these key items:

1. Is the verb tense accurate?
2. Is the spelling correct?
3. Is the white space is easily identifiable?
4. Is it no more than one or two pages for entry level, two to three pages for a mid-level manager and no more than four or five pages for an executive?

5. Is it structured neatly and easy on the eyes?

6. Is it printed on plain 8.5 inch by 11 inch printer paper?

Our resume support team has a long history working in human resources and on recruitment and staffing teams across a variety of industries. We set up our resumes to efficiently highlight your assets, experience and accomplishments. The resume we develop for you shows how you can contribute to the company.

Resume Preparation Guidelines

Hiring managers read about 7-10 seconds into a resume, before they decide which of three piles to place it in: A (strongly consider), B (might consider) and C (would not consider). So you must write your resume to get into pile "A" then get an interview. Naturally, the area at the top of a resume gets the most eye traffic. Make your summary a 3-5 line description of your background, highlighting your key skills.

When defining a position, quantify the statement with percentages and sales numbers. For a sales position: "I consistently exceeded my sales goal by over 120 percent in the past 3 years". For an operations management position: "I reduced expenses 30 percent by streamlining operations and more efficient staff management". Companies want to hire people who can make an important and immediate impact.

General Rule of Thumb

Remember the 3 C's: clear, concise and consistent. Use correct spelling, grammar and punctuation. Be professional.

Not only do misspellings and misuse of grammar and punctuation make you look bad, but it makes you look like you don't pay attention to detail. Employers want people who do pay attention to detail! Use spellcheck before you save your resume. "Technician" is not spelled with two T's! But also remember that spellcheck programs won't find word usage errors. Ask a friend or family member to review the resume, too, for errors you might overlook.

Font Size and Style

Set your name in type between 12 and 14 points, possibly larger or smaller depending on the font you use. Make the address slightly smaller than your name; 11 or 12 points is best. Don't make the resume body text smaller than 11 points. Never use "Courier," the font style that mimics an old-style typewriter.

School Names

Be exact, as there are schools with similar names. If the official name of the school is "The Catholic University of America, Columbus School of Law," refer to it as such.

Italics and Titles

Refer to a style guide, such as "The Chicago Manual of Style" for guidance on when to italicize titles of articles, books, and other publications. Don't italicize Latin phrases commonly used in legal writing such as Juris Doctor, cum laude, et al., etc.

GPA and Rank

Include your grade-point average if you're in the top half of your class or above 3.0. Provide GPA and class rank, such as valedictorian, or just rank if you prefer. For some employers, GPA alone isn't informative enough, but if you don't in the top half of your class and wish to include your GPA, you can. Since it tends to raise a red flag, be cautious about using GPA for just courses in your major, or mentioning grades in single courses, unless you also include your overall GPA. Use the GPA and rank provided by the school.

Abbreviations

Abbreviate states using postal codes, without periods. Be consistent with all abbreviations.

Spell out months of employment. Spell out degrees, but take into account the entire resume's style and if you have enough space.

Bullets

Bullets are best used if you're lacking in experience or have used short sentences to describe positions that may be choppy when read in paragraph form.

Bullets aren't suitable for an individual who has considerable information to relate and needs to fit it on a single page. In that case, a narrative in paragraph format, with tasks separated by semicolons, works well.

When using bullets, don't use periods at the end of each bullet phrase unless it's a complete sentence. Allow two to three spaces between the bullet symbol and the beginning of the text. Recommended types of bullets include filled-in circles or squares.

Order of Employment Information

List job positions in reverse chronological order. Put the most recent job first.

Place the employer's name and location on the first line, at the left margin. On the second line, put your job title and dates of employment. For example:

Coca-Cola Bottling Company, Atlanta, GA
Trademark Specialist, March-August 1995

Sometimes the use of a season (e.g., "Fall") is preferable to listing the months, such as "September to December," when listing employment during school.

For each job, list your "Reason for leaving." Especially if you were laid off or downsized, put this after the company name, job title, or location.

Technical Skills

Avoid specifying "Microsoft Office" and "Windows Operating System." These are too vague; each has different components and versions. Instead, be more specific: "Microsoft Word, Excel, PowerPoint, Outlook" and "Windows 8."

"Interests"

Interests that reflect leadership qualities, dedication to a single cause or hobby, or a unique accomplishment makes a noteworthy contribution to a resume. It's better to have fewer interests that show a theme rather than a slew of general entries.

For instance, "10K Race Participant" is better than "Running.").

"Objective" and "References"

Don't include either of these categories in your resume. Place your "Objective" in your cover letter. Don't list "References" or state "References available upon request." It's commonly understood that references can be provided.

Keywords

Use keywords likely to be used by any recruiter or hiring manager searching computer databases for candidates. Use universal verbiage that can be placed into any scanning system, and contains specific job titles that the hiring companies are targeting.

Subject and Verb Tense

The subject of your resume is "I," first person grammatically. This is understood, so don't include the word "I." Rather than stating, "I conduct new hire orientations," simply say, "Conduct new hire orientations."

Never speak in the third person, such as, "Conducts new hire orientations." In that sentence the subject is understood as, "John conducts new hire orientations." The correct statement is, "Conduct new hire orientations." The subject "I" is understood.

If you're describing your responsibilities and tasks from a past job, use past tense, such as "developed." If describing a present job, use present tense: "develop."

Action Words for Resumes and Cover Letters

These words are all in past tense. Change them to present tense if you're describing a current job.

My resume clients are grateful to be guided through a strategic, sometimes intellectually labor-intensive, process that helps them FOCUS on targeted goals.

In fact, the more targeted you are in your search, the more attractive you are to hiring influencers, decision makers and recruiters. Slow down, put on your blinders to whose advice you are heeding, and conduct a well-thought-out job search.

Note: Don't pay more than $75 for a resume! Career coaches write resumes in less than 90 minutes.

S

Social Networking

"By giving people the power to share, we're making the world more transparent." — Mark Zuckerberg

The Social Networking Trifecta: LinkedIn, Facebook and Twitter

If you're not a member already, you need to join what I call "The Social Networking Trifecta." It consists of LinkedIn, Facebook and Twitter. You're probably asking yourself, "Do I really need to be on ALL of them?" The answer is: Yes. Why? Because everyone else is! Also, different people have different preferences on which of these social media is their "favorite" to use. Some people may think Facebook is more user-friendly than LinkedIn. Others may find they get more activity on Twitter than on Facebook. Whatever the case, you must be a part of them all. They all serve the same key purpose: to connect, share information and maintain relations with a growing network of people.

But there are some important differences.

1. LinkedIn is a business network designed to help professionals find jobs, people, and service providers. It's primarily used by co-workers and business colleagues. Similar to an online resume, your profile contains education and work history and contact information. The main function LinkedIn doesn't have, and that Facebook and Twitter do, is the ability to update your status and provide new messages.

2. Facebook is an online social networking

directory that connects people with friends and others who work, study and live around them. People use Facebook to keep up with friends, upload photos, share links and videos, and learn more about the people they meet. It originally started as a site strictly for colleges and universities.

3. Twitter is a free website that blends social networking with the ability to post short messages or micro-blogs limited to 140 characters or less. These are commonly known as "tweets." Tweets are designed to be accessed on mobile devices and through the Internet, where they're posted to the user's personal Web page. This can be restricted to select viewers, or viewed by anyone. Unlike instant messaging, viewers don't reply to Twitter postings. Unlike LinkedIn and Facebook, Twitter doesn't display your personal information.

In addition to friends, families and working professionals, the Trifecta sites have quickly become a networking staple for the media, politics, companies, businesses, the sports world and celebrities.

Social networking sites have changed the way we network. Real-time networking made possible by these sites has shortened the gap between finding opportunity and taking action. You can find and apply for jobs faster than ever. They allow you to maintain a network bigger than ever! But it's how you use your contacts that counts. You can have 500 friends on Facebook, but if you never reach out to them, how can you benefit?

Like employment history, education and experience on a resume, your profile, connections and status advance you on social sites. The key to success on these sites is staying frequent and relevant.

Once you've created your profiles, include URL links to your LinkedIn, Facebook and Twitter pages in your email signature. If people have this information at their fingertips, they're more likely to use it.

LinkedIn

Get Linking

1. Connect to everyone you know, so you can connect to who they know.

    A. Search the schools you attended (including high school). Even if people don't remember you, most classmates will connect with you anyway to grow their network.

    B. Search the places you've worked and add everyone with whom you had a good working experience. You can ask them to give you LinkedIn Recommendations that make your profile more attractive.

2. Join professional groups on LinkedIn relating to your current or desired profession. This is a great way to find out about events and job opportunities.

3. Create a target list of ten to twenty companies based on your research and advice from friends, former co-workers and other members of professional and alumni groups. Use the company filter to search for people in your direct or indirect network who work at your target companies. Connect with them, tell them about your interest in working there and why you are a good fit. Find out what professional associations their industry has and join them. When you contact these people, mention that you belong to the same association.

LinkedIn Advanced Searching Tips

To the left of the main Search field, click the drop-down menu and make a selection (People, Jobs, Groups, etc.) Click "Advanced" next to the Search field.
Search Type
What To Use
Examples

Boolean search:
Use AND or OR, or both using parentheses.
Use a minus sign (-) to eliminate a word from search results.
Place quotation marks around two-plus word phrases, such as "Technical Writer.")
Examples:
Manager AND Executive
Admin OR Administrative
(Tech OR Technical) AND Writer
Facility OR Office — Hospital

Reference search
Select "Search People" from the drop-down, click "Advanced."
Click "Reference Search" tab. Enter Company Name and Years.

Find people's profiles
Search Google, Yahoo and Bing:
site:*www.linkedin.com (COMPANY1 OR COMPANY2)* -inurl:static -inurl:redirect
site:*www.linkedin.com* KEYWORD1 COMPANY1 -inurl:jobId
site:*www.linkedin.com* (Google OR Motorola) -inurl:static -inurl:redirect

site:*www.linkedin.com* C++ Google -
inurl:jobId

**Find people's profiles from non-LinkedIn
sites**

Search Google, Yahoo and Bing:
linkdomain:*www.linkedin.com*
(KEYWORD1 OR KEYWORD2) JOBTITLE1
linkdomain:*www.linkedin.com* (Sarbanes
OR sox) analyst

Connect to power networkers
Conduct a search where your only criterion
is a target industry or company, and sort by the
number of connections. Connect to those with the
most connections.

Facebook

Facebook isn't just another social
networking site for friends. The need for many
people to find new employment, and the fast rate at
which Facebook is growing globally, are reasons
why even working professionals are joining.
Individuals, companies and recruiters now use
Facebook for candidate searching and job-hunting.

Making the Most of Facebook in Your Job Search

1. Don't put anything on your profile that
you don't want your future boss to see. Make sure
all the information is valid and matches your
LinkedIn and Twitter profiles.
2. Complete your profile so it matches your
resume. Even though Facebook may not seem like a
traditional way to search for candidates, recruiters
are still looking for the traditional information about
candidates: their personality traits,

accomplishments, education history and dates, employment history and dates, volunteer work, memberships and associations.

3. Make your profile photo a nice, professional headshot. Delete all unprofessional and "incriminating" photos. Even if they haven't met you face to face, your online photo gives a recruiter the first impression. Post photos of yourself doing community service, participating in sporting events, conducting speeches or conferences, working at church fundraisers, teaching or reading to kids, helping animals, helping the elderly, traveling — learning about new cultures— anything employers look upon positively!

4. You can be professional and interesting at the same time. Let your true personality shine through in your profile. Show your humorous, fun-loving self; just keep it clean and non-offensive! Employers want fun employees; they don't want sarcastic, rude or over-opinionated employees.

5. Let people know you're looking for a new job. So many people are on Facebook, and so many people are looking for work, that this is no longer an issue. The people in your network want to help you, because they want you to help them if they lose their jobs. Update your status to show everyone how you're actively seeking work: making copies of your resume, meeting with recruiters, interviewing—but don't say with whom. People love to see what others are doing. That's why the "What are you doing?" exists! They also love to comment. The more comments you get, the better. It shows that people are interested in you. Your updates may prompt referrals and recommendations.

6. Show your knowledge to your network.

Just like updating your status, this is an indirect method to attract your network to your skills and expertise in your chosen industry. By sharing interesting information and links on your Wall, you can build up a profile as a knowledge expert in your industry. It shows you're passionate and interested in your industry, and serious about presenting yourself in the right way.

7. In addition to searching Facebook for people from different industries and schools, try tools like *Wink.com*, which search locations and industries on Facebook profiles. Use relevant keywords, job titles, brand names and buzzwords from your target industries. Become their friends, keep in contact with them and find relevant friends in their networks.

8. Join relevant professional groups on Facebook. These are a great entry point to meet people with similar interests. They want to share information and experiences with you; that's what the groups are for.

9. Actively engage and share information with people. Get involved with the conversations going on within your network, as shown on your news feed. Add some opinion and meaningful answers. This helps build credibility and presence and shows that you care. Ask questions, too. That helps start conversation and encourages responses. If people who don't know you personally see this, the first thing they do is read your profile. The more people look at your profile, the more they'll have you in mind, which is good for when a job comes up.

10. Grow your network to obtain more secondary and third-level contacts. These people can get you a job just as easily as a first-level

contact; it's all about the people they know. In your job search, finding people on Facebook, LinkedIn and Twitter need to be a regular function: targeting relevant people and expanding your professional, not social, network.

Twitter

Twitter is growing rapidly. The main reason for Twitter's growth is the ease of sharing and finding information on a second-by-second basis. It's fast-paced, quick-hitting and gets relevant information to your followers in an instant. Employers are using Twitter and other social networking sites to research job applicants. Therefore, as a job-seeker, you need to know how to use Twitter in your job search.

Here is how you can use Twitter daily:

1. Maintaining and expanding your personal brand
2. Managing your followers and who you're following
3. Researching
4. Helping yourself by helping others

How & Why?

Researching companies, their products, and services.
Leads to
Finding a job!

Sharing relevant and interesting news, articles and insights for your chosen profession and industry.
Leads to
Finding a job!

Building a following, credibility and influence that can be leveraged into direct contacts within companies.

Leads to

Finding a job!

Top 10 Benefits

1. Stand out from other job-seekers. Show you're "in the loop" and really involved in your industry and job search.

2. Prove your industry experience and expertise, based on your "Tweets," your followers and following, and your re-Tweets—circulating other Tweets.

3. Develop your personal brand as a subject matter expert who's connected with industry leaders.

4. Update your followers on the progress of your job search.

5. Connect with management, employees and owners of companies that you're interested in working with to build a relationship before inquiring about job openings. Follow all the people you find interesting, and those from your industry, who might be able to help you at some stage in your job search.

6. Build, grow, and maintain relationships with your personal and professional network, which includes current and former co-workers, clients, vendors, referrals and other industry contacts.

7. Know the companies you're interested in working with, through research about their products, industry, management, employees, projects and news. This will help you decide whether you want to work there or not. If you do, you can also use this information during your

interview.

8. Research the companies and publish your findings. When job-hunting, you need to research no matter what. Instead of just keeping the information to yourself, you can publish it, making it available to others, including the people who are going to hire you. Many job-seekers are hired just because they know more about social media and the company than people inside the company do. Show you know about them, and that you're serious about working there.

9. It's easy! Twitter only allows 140 characters per post, so you don't spend a lot of time writing, or racking your brain to find something to write. Not to mention that people are more likely to read a small amount of information than a long article. Finding and posting or re-Tweeting relevant and interesting articles, tips, tricks, news, and information is easy to do and very rewarding.

10. It's fun! Twitter and other social networking sites wouldn't have caught on if they were difficult and boring!

Twitter-Related Sites and Tools

Tool Name	Website
AdF.ly	*adf.ly*

Pays you for visits to your blogs and/or Tweets. Make sure they're worthy of being passed on and relevant to your industry knowledge. Post all the articles you created on Blogger, then take each article link on Blogger and shrink it in AdF.ly. Take that shrunken link in AdF.ly and post to Twitter. When people click the shrunken link on Twitter, it redirects them to the Blogger site where the article is. You make money doing this!

Bit.ly

bit.ly

Shortens URL links. If you use TweetDeck, Bit.ly is automatically enabled. If not, you have to be able to manage your 140 characters wisely to get your point across. If you're sending a link, the URL alone could be 300 characters. Bit.ly and others like TinyUrl, Adf.ly, etc. shrink your link to a manageable size. Great for Twitter link posters.

Twello
www.Twello.com
TwitDir
www.TwitDir.com

Twitter directories where you can find other industry professionals who are on Twitter and who they are following.

TweetDeck
www.TweetDeck.com

Manage your screen, groups and feeds coming into and out of your Twitter home page. Leverage unique search features and track specific people you're looking to connect with. TweetDeck manages everything live on your screen and runs in the background.

Twhirl
www.Twhirl.org

Manage your following and respond to your followers. You can create groups to follow, which is great if you're interested in several different types of jobs or careers.

Twitterberry (for Blackberry)
www.orangatame.com/products/twitterberry
Twitterific (for iPhone*)
iconfactory.com/software/twitterific
Mobile Twitter (all cellulars) *m.twitter.com*

Access Twitter on the go from your mobile device. It mobilizes your job search! But please, don't use your mobile device while driving!

*If you have an iPhone, here are some great job-related apps: 100 Words to Make You Sound Smart, beamME CV, Craigster, iJobs, JobCompass and TwitterFon.

TwitterSearch
search.twitter.com
TwitterSearch has its own language but it is easy to pick up and performs a more specific search than the normal search feature in Twitter.

Monitter
www.monitter.com
Search using keywords and see who's mentioning these words in their tweets. It has an advanced search feature. You can RSS your subjects, company or even yourself.
Don't forget to use these words in some searches: job, hiring, recruiter, recruiting. Search commonly used words that industry people are using too.

TweetBeep
tweetbeep.com
Create alerts for Twitter and receive them via email. Very similar to Google Alerts.

TweetScan
tweetscan.com
TweetScan searches Twitter, identi.ca and other Status.net-based sites. You can search public messages and user profiles with results available via email, RSS, and JSON. Find lost or multi-user replies. Scan up to 10 phrases for daily or weekly delivery. No ads or spam.

TwitHire
twithire.com
Free job board for Twitter. Currently it has four separate categories.

Twitter Feed

twitterfeed.com

Use to help build links back to you. If you're a blogger, this is a great tool to blast your posts to your Twitter followers as you publish. It's real-time and effective.

TwittURLy
twitturly.com

Find out about the top URLs being talked about and tracked on the web.

Getting Started with Twitter
1. Sign up.
2. Build your profile. Link to Facebook so that when you post a tweet, it automatically gets posted on your Facebook page.
3. Start following other people with your job title.
4. Follow your interests and industries.
5. Follow friends, co-workers, recruiters, experts, websites, news, etc.
6. Start sending messages and "tweets." Avoid sharing trivial information, like what you ate for breakfast. Share relevant, useful information regarding your expertise, industry, job search status, etc. This goes for Facebook too.

Twitter Commands
Command: Result

@username + message: Directs a tweet at another person and causes your tweet to save in their "Direct Messages". Example: "@candidate do you want to hear about a job opening with MJW Careers?"

D username + message: Sends a person a private message that goes to their device and saves in their web archive

WHOIS username: Retrieves the profile information for any public user on Twitter

GET username: Retrieves the latest twitter update posted by that person

NUDGE username: Reminds a friend to update

FAV username: Marks a person's last tweet as a favorite

#: Use the number sign or hash tag (#) in front of keywords. When people like potential employers search for these words on Twitter, your tweet, and therefore your resume, appears.

Search Engine Optimization (SEO)

Unfortunately, with today's online hiring and recruitment practices, some of the older job search methods, like only posting your resume on a job board like Monster, do not cut it anymore.

Effectively stand out by creating and managing an online presence that puts your name at the top of the recruiters' search results. How? Search engine optimization, or SEO. Large companies and organizations have used SEO techniques for years to develop their brands and reputations. When you do the same, when hiring managers search, they can easily find you and find information that represents you as the best person to hire.

1. Perform a search on yourself and delete anything you don't want a potential employer to see. Most hiring managers search names as an online reference check for candidates during the interviewing process. Failing to delete your "digital dirt" can seriously weaken your chances for a job offer. Also, it takes a lot of time to build your online brand by maintaining a website or blog. Don't let

any dirt ruin all your time and hard work.

2. Buy your domain name. Go to a domain registrar like *GoDaddy.com* and buy a variation of your name. That might be first and last; first, middle initial and, last; first, middle and last. Establish a website and/or blog. Design the site and develop content for it. It's easy to download website templates online. Many web hosting companies offer these as part of their inexpensive do-it-yourself site-building packages. Or hire a web designer to develop your site's look and feel. Make sure to choose an option that lets you easily and quickly update and add content to your site. At a minimum, include:

A. Home page with your contact information, mission statement, elevator speech, short bio and a professional, polished photo.

B. Current version of your resume.

C. Portfolio with samples of your best work, reflecting your unique talents and skills.

D. Video resume or portfolio that serves as a "pre-interview." Attract hiring managers by introducing yourself with a quality, 2-3 minute presentation.

E. Additional content such as articles, tips, video or audio clips and photographs that demonstrate your industry knowledge and expertise.

F. A page of links with valuable websites related to your professional and personal interests. Some of the sites may not link back to you, but having them on your site still increases your search engine ranking.

3. Research keywords and key phrases for your field and include them on your website. Find the keywords and phrases that employers in your

field use to refer to the job you are seeking. Keywords include job titles, company names, skill sets, industry buzzwords and jargon, certification names, software titles, etc. Look for these keywords in job postings at your present and desired level. The best places to use keywords are your elevator speech, bio, resume, online portfolio, blog entries and articles. Don't "force" or overuse keywords, but do try to incorporate them in titles and in the beginning and ending paragraphs of any article or page.

    4. Write relevant articles for your site or other sites. Search engines love high-quality content that adds value to the Internet, especially when other sites link to it, which reinforces that value. As a job-seeker, developing content that showcases your knowledge and expertise raises your value in the employment marketplace. For example, write an article for an online industry publication or blog. Or submit your article to one of many online article sites such as *EzineArticles.com, WordPress.com, PubArticles.com, EHow.com, BizSugar.com, Digg.com, ArticleDirectory.com*, and *GoArticles.com*.

    5. Maximize use of keywords in web page titles and Meta tags. Meta tags are tools are used by search engines to understand, classify, and describe each of your pages in search results. Use keywords and Meta tags in your pages' title, site description, and body text.

    6. Advertise your site. Add your website or blog URL to everything! Even if your site isn't perfect or complete, list it on anything that includes your name: email signatures, resume, business cards, and when you post content or comments on other blogs or user forums. Using social

networking, invite your friends to visit your site and offer you constructive feedback how you can improve it. Ask other sites to link to yours, to increase its visibility and ranking. List links to the personal sites of your friends, family, and colleagues. Ask them to reciprocate with links back to your site. Submit your site to search engines, databases and directories including Google, Yahoo and Bing.

T

Turning to Someone for Help

"A smart person is someone who can take a complex issue and make it simple." — Anonymous

Career Coaching Services

We offer career coaching services for companies and universities, including:

1. Resume writing & critique: Allows employers to review your assets and accomplishments, while maintaining brevity. We also provide a critique of your current resume.

2. Cover letter preparation: Interchangeable to the exact position for any employer, right down to how you can provide a solution to their needs, making your knowledge appear superior to your competitor.

3. Follow-up letter preparation: While you're still fresh in the hiring manager's mind, you need to act quickly. We provide an effective follow-up letter that shows why you can be the solution to an employer's human capital needs.

4. Customized career assessment: When you know what career you want and how to get it, your chances of getting and interview and getting hired increase considerably. Find a career you enjoy! This service also includes a free salary report.

5. Interview training: Step-by-step instruction on managing your job interview strategy, from the initial call to post-interview steps.

6. Mock interview sessions: A great tool to understanding the interviewing process. Answer the most difficult questions, ask the right questions and

ease the fear of interviewing forever. Eliminate the competition and secure more job offers.

7. One-on-one career consulting: Includes one hour of personal assessment and discussion on such topics as unemployment benefits, finding temp work, budgeting, goal setting, retirement planning and meal planning.

8. JobStickers services: Newsletter and social networking site enrollment.

9. Career seminars enrollment: Every month, one of our industry experts hosts a live phone seminar to discuss career insights and techniques.

10. Job-hunting techniques: As you know, job-hunting is a job in and of itself. New methods, techniques for the Internet and career fairs, first-hand knowledge of job search tools, are saturating the hidden job market, and more. This service also includes a free cost of living calculation.

11. Internet as a source: In today's career search, the Internet is vital. Includes four services: Internet resume posting consultation, Internet job search, Internet marketing and Internet research.

12. Self-marketing training: We show you how to promote yourself effectively, to stand out among increasing competition in the workforce.

13. Networking training: "It's not what you know, but who you know." Let us show you how to get the most out of networking.

14. Job-loss counseling: Transition assistance and advice about turning job loss into a learning and self-improvement opportunity.

15. Career-focused contact management: We find contact information for employers who are hiring so you know who to contact directly.

16. Job search work team implementation:

Placing your similar employees together on their job-hunt.

Why MJW Careers Outplacement Program?

The major influencers on the client company's choice to purchase our outplacement services are:

1. Improved employee morale, motivation and productivity

A full 66 percent of employers surveyed believe outplacement support improves morale, motivation and productivity during times of change for current employees not affected directly by a layoff (Reed Consulting survey). Recent research shows a correlation between declines in work performance and the negative climate produced by layoffs—often referred to as "layoff survivor syndrome." Layoffs not only create stress for workers who are laid off, but also for those co-workers who remain behind (Sirota Survey Intelligence).

2. Improved retention and boomerang hiring

When a company wants to rehire a previous employee, it needs to make sure there's no bad taste in the prospect's mouth. Data shows 25 percent of laid-off employees eventually returned to their old jobs, while 33 percent would consider returning (Enterprise Rent-A-Car and YouGov surveys). Among employers, 65 percent of those surveyed agree that providing outplacement support for exiting staff helps retain remaining staff (Reed Consulting survey). Two more surveys showed that 38 percent of employers have indicated they anticipate some type of recall of cut workers (Department of Labor) and that 18 percent of laid-off workers in 2009 who landed new positions were rehired by the employer that let them go, up from 13 percent in 2005 (R.I.G.H.T. Management Report.) A positive for boomerang hiring is that it will include savings for the employer on recruiting and training costs, the benefits of maintaining former associations between customers and employees, and the fact that the rehired employee doesn't need an introduction to his or her colleagues.

3. Improved reputation and brand protection
Of employers surveyed, 78 percent believe providing outplacement could improve the organization's reputation (Reed Consulting Survey).

4. Enhanced public relations
Providing outplacement support can boost your overall ratings in the media and among investors.

5. Minimize unemployment insurance payments
The support an employee receives can in turn create opportunities to get employment faster, which will take the employee off unemployment insurance that the company is paying for.

6. Employer of choice
A majority of employers, 55 percent of those surveyed, believe outplacement can help the organization be seen as an employer of choice (Reed Consulting survey).

7. Reduction in legal action and avoiding future litigation
Providing outplacement reduces employers' legal liability, 69 percent of those surveyed believe. Employees feel better about their employer if they are given assistance during their transition, which reduces the risk of termination lawsuits (SHRM & Gale Group Study). Types of lawsuits that can be

avoided include unfair dismissal, anti-discrimination, age discrimination, wages and hours and employment discrimination.

8. Future customers and alliance partners.

A quarter of those HR personnel surveyed said they view former employers as potential future customers (SHRM & Gale Group Study) or alliance partners.

9. Union mandate

Unions or other organized associations are now mandating outplacement as a part of a severance package, according to 5 percent of HR personnel surveyed (SHRM & Gale Group Study).

10. Stress reduction for management

Of more than 1,200 HR executives in North America, 66 percent said outplacement reduces stress on managers making organizational changes, which makes their jobs easier (SHRM & Gale Group Study). It also minimizes the level of discomfort for both the displaced employee and the company. Since the economy took the plunge, more than 50 percent of managers have reported stress-related symptoms (U.S.'s EAP company, ComPsych). Leon Grunberg, a sociologist at the University of Puget Sound who conducted a long-term job stress study among managers, reported that managers were reporting stress symptoms up to 3 years after layoffs took place.

11. Government regulatory and compliance

Of HR Professionals surveyed, 14 percent say they offer outplacement services to comply with layoff legislation (SHRM & Gale Group Study). A number of states are passing laws improving employee protections.

Many business leaders are tracking the long list of potential labor-friendly (aka "business-hostile") initiatives and litigation trends. These include an expected increase in audit and enforcement activity by the U.S. Department of Labor, the Equal Employment Opportunity Commission, and other state and federal agencies, made possible by increased funding; proposals for mandatory paid medical leave and required health and welfare benefits; more equal pay discrimination claims based on the recently passed Lilly Ledbetter Fair Pay Act; a seemingly endless uptick in individual and class-action lawsuits, as millions of laid-off employees explore their options with emboldened plaintiff's attorneys; and the resurgence of organized labor in the private sector, regardless of the final form of the Employee Free Choice Act (Newsweek).

An additional law is the WARN Act (Worker Adjustment and Retraining Notification). This offers protection to workers, their families and communities by requiring employers to provide notice 60 days in advance of covered plant closings and covered mass layoffs. This notice must be provided to either affected workers or their representatives (i.e., a labor union); to the state's dislocated worker unit; and to the appropriate unit of local government. WARN applies to businesses with at least 100 workers. Notices are required for layoffs of 50 or more employees at one "employment site" within a 30-day period if those employees represent one-third of the work force. WARN is also required for any layoff of 500 or more workers. An employer that has violated the act is liable to the affected employees for back pay and benefits for the period of the violation, generally 60 days. An employee can bring a lawsuit in federal court and, in recent years, some employees have brought class actions under the WARN Act.

Another law is the Forewarn Act (Federal Oversight, Reform and Enforcement of the WARN Act,) that is strengthening current federal law due to the massive increase in layoffs. The Forewarn Act strengthens the employee notification process for mass layoffs or plant closing and add tools to enforce the current WARN Act, which became law in 1988. Unfortunately, few employers are abiding by the WARN Act. According to the Government Accountability Office, only one-third of employers are providing this notification. The Forewarn Act would give the U.S. Department of Labor (DOL) and state attorneys general the authority to enforce the WARN Act. The Forewarn Act would:

A. Increase penalties to double back pay plus benefits

B. Reduce the mass layoff figure from 50 to 25

C. Reduce the covered employer size from 100 to 50 employees

D. Lengthen the notification period from 60 to 90 days

E. Require employers to provide written notification to the Department of Labor

This legislation would clearly add protections for those workers who are about to lose their jobs due to mass layoffs or plant closings. The new requirement of providing written notification to the DOL would force employers to be more forthright and public with their downsizings. The new financial penalties for non-compliance will likely spur employers to comply (CCH Aspen Publishers Technical Answer Group).

12. Social media

We incorporate the use of social media and

Web 2.0 tools in all programs.

U

Undercover Job-seekers

"You are never too old to set another goal or to dream a new dream." — C. S. Lewis

Job-hunting While Employed

My dad always said, "Don't ever stop looking for a job!" He's right. Keeping your options open and being active in the job market is smart for everyone. Unfortunately, no one's job is ever "safe." Whether you've worked somewhere two years or thirty, administrative or executive, job loss is always a possibility. There was a time when employees stayed with an employer for a long time, typically twenty or thirty years. Unfortunately, times have changed and such longevity is no longer an option for the majority of today's workforce.

Being ready for a potential job loss makes an actual job loss much easier, emotionally and professionally. Even if you don't lose your job, you may just find a better job than the one you have now.

Maybe you're not happy with your current job. Maybe it's not challenging enough or there's no possibility to advance. While many unemployed might love to have your job, we've all been in a place where we just want to get out and move on. Being proactive may help you get where you want to be.

If you're job-hunting while employed, you have three goals: 1) maintain your current job, 2) devote time to find a new job, and 3) not let your current employer find out you're looking to leave the company.

The following steps help you create the discretion you need to meet these goals.

1. Update your current role on your resume so potential employers know what you are currently doing. Provide only your personal phone number and email address, not your work information.

2. Be mindful where you post your resume online, so your current employer doesn't see it. Use the "hide my contact information" and other confidentiality features for your profile.

3. Don't list your current manager as a reference! Use only previous employers.

4. Talk to people in your network, but be discerning. Let them know you're still employed and are just proactively seeking a new opportunity.

5. Don't look for work while at work! Your boss might overhear something or notice frequent trips to conference rooms or to your car. Do this after work or on weekends.

6. Schedule interviews before or after work, so you're not missing work. Potential employers appreciate you mentioning that you can't interview on company time; it shows your respect for your profession and company.

7. Tell the interviewer that you wish to remain confidential and for them not to contact anyone at your current position.

8. Never bash your current or previous employer during interviews.

9. Don't tell ANY of your current colleagues you're searching for a new job, even your "best friends" you think are trustworthy.

10. If you contact a former boss or co-worker for help in finding a new job, make sure they respect your confidentiality. Don't ask for help

from former colleagues who might know or speak with your current colleagues.

11. When speaking to potential employers, promote your capability, not so much your availability.

12. Continue to self-market. Share your expertise by writing on your own blog, industry blogs and articles in industry publications and websites, and by speaking at industry conferences.

13. Don't check out mentally. After deciding they want to get new job, some people tend to slow down or show a bad attitude, which can hurt them when seeking new opportunities.

14. Keep up the hard work, focus and maintain a positive attitude at your current job!

V

Victory

"You can learn a line from a win and a book from a defeat." — Paul Brown

I want to share some Q&A from some successful HR professionals about the employment process.

QUESTION: I'm interested in transitioning out of financial services into another field. How do I move to another field such as health care without having the experience? Most positions require experience.

ANSWER: You need to leverage your functional expertise. For example, if you are a technology professional, position yourself to sell your technical knowledge and how it relates to the desired new industry. Identify contacts within your network who can help introduce you to your target companies. Begin to network within the industry by attending related professional association meetings, join LinkedIn Groups and watch the dialogue to understand what's on the minds of professionals within this new targeted industry. Attend seminars, speakers and other related events to build up your knowledge of the industry "speak." It will help you when talking with hiring managers. Consider trying to work your way in through an agency on a temporary basis so the company gets to know you. Consider volunteering some of your time within the industry. This will put you on the path to future opportunities within your targeted industry. As the market becomes more robust, the request for specific industry experience will lighten up.

QUESTION: If someone is unemployed for more than two years, do you feel that person is too lazy to get a job? Or is it just their bad luck?

ANSWER: I wouldn't automatically think a person is lazy due to many factors. The person could have returned to college, or working as a volunteer at an organization, or maybe was working part-time, or has heath issues. The point is that every person has various reasons for why they're unemployed. I personally have known several friends who remained unemployed a year or two. It was very challenging for them to find work, and they were applying, networking, going on interviews like crazy and had Masters Degrees. So I wouldn't ever think someone is lazy, but rather give them the opportunity to state their case and the factors around their long-term unemployment. I agree with it being a case-by-case scenario. Every career, background, industry and overall character comes into play. I think that if people truly exert themselves each day towards their goal, they will achieve it. Two years is a long time, but it doesn't mean the candidate is lazy. They need to adjust their itinerary and calendar to better allocate time and resources so they eliminate this prolonged employment gap.

QUESTION: I have a candidate interested in putting her church volunteer work on her LinkedIn profile, but am wondering how to do it without being taboo or offending others?

ANSWER: In a word, relevance. If it relates to a specific job she is applying for, then yes, include it on her resume, be proud of what she did and why, and no one should take offense. On the flip side, while I support individualism, everyone needs to be sensitive to the diverse community in which they choose to work. Championing any cause may not always be suitable for the workplace. Unless that workplace is "cause specific," you run the risk of upsetting somebody, somewhere. If the church volunteering on her resume is as far as it goes, I cannot see why anybody would get upset, though you know somebody will. If she is appointed and brings the church volunteering into the work environment where it's not welcome on a regular basis, and someone gets offended, this would not be acceptable. I could share many horrible stories where non-relevant championed causes were brought into the workplace and caused a tidal wave of unnecessary upset.

QUESTION: Is your "elevator pitch" really THAT important?? In most interviews, you have to be prepared for a thirty-minute to an hour-long conversation with a hiring manager. What if you have less than 5 minutes to convince a hiring employer that you're the most qualified candidate?

ANSWER: Of course! What the heck is two hours of your time to sit down, evaluate yourself and write up a quick thirty-second blurb on who you are, what you do and what you're trying to do? Unless you're a gabber or an improvisational guru, you might want to memorize something, purely for the sake of not tripping up. Who knows who you meet who can impact your livelihood. Don't sound robotic, but don't look like blockhead, either. You cannot remain shortsighted. And if you're solely talking about an interview scenario? That's a no-brainer to me. Do *everything* you can in your control. This question never sits well with me.

QUESTION: I'm in the process of transition from the HR field in the military. I'm trying to get my foot in the HR in the civilian sector. I'm thinking about taking an information technology course. Will that help me with getting a job?

ANSWER: This is hugely important to gain and maintain credibility. Make sure you translate your resume to civilian terms and do the same in interviews. For example, talk about "projects" and "plans" instead of "missions." At best, the military terms can be confusing for the corporate world, and may make your experience seem less relevant. Also, learn what you can about areas that you don't have experience with, perhaps benefits or workers' compensation. Connect with HR groups in your local area. The Society of Human Resources (SHRM) should list the local chapters on their website.

W

Watching Your Goals and Spending

"What keeps me going is goals." —
Muhammad Ali

It's a good idea not to get carried away once
your life is in transition. That's true of eating,
drinking, spending, etc. A smart way to approach
your new life is to set some goals and monitor a
budget.

Goals and Objectives Should Be SMARTER

A SMARTER goal or objective is:
Specific: Instead of being general, such as a
goal to improve your work ethic, write something
attainable like "Read the self-help book each day"
and then create a routine to cross off your
achievement each day. I like to use a "Don't Break
the Chain" document, which Jerry Seinfeld used to
help him write standup jokes every day.
Measurable: Now that you've implemented
a specific goal, make it attainable. Instead of "Read
the self-help book each day," make it "read five
pages of the self-help book each day."
Acceptable: Make sure you set a goal that
you know can get accomplished. Don't take on
more goals than you can handle. This is similar to
not living outside your financial means. It's a good
idea to be the goal-setter in this scenario.
Realistic: Making the goal realistic is, in
essence, to ensure you aren't going to "Read five
pages of the self-help book in under one minute."
So ensure you give yourself a time frame that

doesn't weigh you down or isn't logically possible.

Time frame: Give yourself ample time to complete your goal, but also make sure you don't make it impossible for you. A good tip here is not to procrastinate. If the book you're reading is in-depth and so technically heavy that you may have to jot notes as you read, it's a good idea to either start at the beginning of your day or space the task out throughout the day. Having to get your reading done ten minutes before bedtime isn't smart.

Extending: If the goal is something you're passionate about or will help improve your situation or knowledge for your long term goals, it will be more attainable. When you face challenges, it's good to learn about solutions that will help you achieve success by extending your capabilities.

Rewarding: Give yourself some incentives, which will make the journey that much more fulfilling. Make sure you space out the rewards, though, so you aren't inclined to regress.

It's smart to use a goal setting worksheet.

Budgeting

It's good practice to set up and use several planning and budgeting tools. I recommend a basic budgeting worksheet, dealing with debt worksheet, bill payment schedule and a monthly budget schedule.

X

X-Factor

"Here's to the crazy ones, the misfits, the rebels, the troublemakers, the round pegs in the square holes ... the ones who see things differently — they're not fond of rules ... You can quote them, disagree with them, glorify or vilify them, but the only thing you can't do is ignore them because they change things ... they push the human race forward, and while some may see them as the crazy ones, we see genius, because the ones who are crazy enough to think that they can change the world, are the ones who do." — Steve Jobs

When competing against other job-seekers, sometimes it comes down to the X-factor. This is that special something you have and others may not. It helps to first identify this factor and then execute a game plan to incorporate it into your job-hunt. To help identify the X-factor, it's a good idea to first understand your industry's practices and what they allow. A teacher might not be able to market herself at a happy hour, while a business professional might routinely gain contacts over drinks. So knowing your boundaries comes first. Then it's a good idea to start thinking outside the box. Approach your job-hunt with a sense of marketing, which goes well beyond just applying for jobs on the job boards. But remember, the type of marketing effort you pursue will depend on your industry, position, company and hiring manager. So tread lightly until you've fully developed your tactic.

Unusual Job-hunting Techniques

You read about people who take extreme measures when seeking employment. Some of them will undertake an aggressive marketing plan. This can be expensive, but might actually land you an interview. Here are some ideas to get you going when trying to create a marketing plan for job-hunting outside the box.

1. People who stand on corners with signs, dressed up in suits. The signs say thing like "Recently laid-off executive ... will work for 401k."

2. People wearing "Please Hire Me" shirts to job interviews.

3. The guy who bought a billboard saying stating "Results Driven Sales & Operations Manager. Visit *Mark4Hire.com.*"

4. The lady who brought in breakfast every morning to a company until they hired her.

5. Putting resumes on car windshields. This works well at golf tournaments.

6. Look for sponsors for local events such as fireworks, Little League teams, and then find the employers at those companies. It's best to target the actual people and not just the jobs. It's a fact that 60 percent of jobs are not advertised.

7. The candidate who networked in high-end stores on Chicago's Michigan Avenue to meet executives. He targeted some of the executives for the company where he wanted to work and was able to find out where they frequented happy hour. He developed some relationships and landed a job this way.

8. The applicant who landed an interview using a ping-pong paddle. The applicant researched a hiring manager on LinkedIn and noticed that the hiring manager had won a ping-pong tournament, so

the candidate sent a ping-pong paddle and a cover letter with ping-pong-related language.

9. The guy who handed out cups of coffee, along with his resume, to commuters at an intersection.

10. The candidate who started a blog about a company and wrote every day about how wonderful the company was and how great they were doing. It landed him a freelance gig with that said company.

11. The guy who used a line from the movie "Office Space" in his cover letter. The letter simply read, "I don't have a problem with my TPS reports."

12. The lady who created her own job. She monitored the employment practices and job openings of a company that had just opened a new division. She saw that they were going to need a certain support position down the road, so she drafted her own requisition, outlining the job requirements. She sent it to the VP in that particular department along with her resume. It landed her a job.

13. One guy wrote a humorous rejection letter, sent it to the hiring manager and said, "Please send back so at least I know you saw my resume." It landed him the job in the company's creative department.

14. Putting a large magnet on your car that displays your personal website, which in turn displays your resume.

15. The lady who puts perfume on her resume. This might work with male hiring managers.

16. The candidate who bought pizzas for a certain department he was targeting, and placed his resume in each pizza box.

17. Someone wrote a press release announcing she had been hired and used it as her cover letter.

18. The lady who put her resume in a balloon.

19. The guy who created a paper airplane out of his resume.

20. Laminated resumes.

21. The lady who wrote her credentials on her shirt and biked around near various office parkways.

22. Using your family and friends. One guy emailed his closest contacts offering them money for anyone who sent him a referral that ultimately landed him a job.

23. One candidate bought ads on Google for names of top advertising executives. When searched their names for press hits, they saw the candidate's ad along with a link back to his own website with his resume and portfolio of previous projects.

24. One guy recorded a music video about hiring him and uploaded it to YouTube.

25. A candidate redesigned a marketing company's entire website the company loved it so much that he got a job.

Pros

1. Good way to stand out and get noticed.

2. Good way to take a chance. Life's short, so sometimes we need to just go for it!

3. Showcases your creativity.

4. Networking avenue. It could lead to more connections.

5. Fun. It could be interesting and memorable for you, and can be an entertaining story

at your next function.

6. Exposure. Who knows, you may wind up on the evening news or in the newspaper.

7. Cheap. It could be an inexpensive way to approach the job-hunt, but that's only if you look for deals and plan your strategy in advance, so you predict all the possible ways you could be spending going forward.

Cons

1. Expensive. Some of these techniques can be costly and the return on investment might not make sense.

2. Time. You could be better off spending time on other aspects of a self-marketing plan, rather than spin your wheels on a guerilla marketing scheme.

3. Turn-off. It might displease some hiring managers.

4. Come back to bite you. It may land you a job, but when co-workers find out about what you did, some of them might not welcome you as a new employee with the warmth you might have received if you took the more traditional route.

5. Higher expectations. The manager may now see you as an asset in marketing, even though you had just one good idea. You might be given added responsibility beyond your initial job description because the manager was impressed with your guerilla marketing strategy.

6. No metrics. There is really no way to track your results from this type of marketing plan, whereas you can see real data with your cold calling and online pursuits.

7. Energy. It can be tiresome keeping up

with your plan.

Y

Younger and Older Job-seekers: The Ends of the Spectrum

"One lives in the hope of becoming a memory." — Antonic Porchia

Entry Level High-Pot

This is aimed at the entry level job-seeker. A young, energetic, flexible, high potential (high-pot), recently graduated candidate, not biased to the workforce, meaning can learn to do things the right way. We've all been there. We've all been at the bottom of the food chain and have had to take jobs that made us question even our own sanity. The bright-eyed graduate who's ready to take on the world can sometimes get a rude awakening. I've come out of interviews so excited to join the company that I paid no mind to the fact this company churns and burns employees at the drop of a hat. It was like the pre-recession mortgage industry, and I don't mean to knock this industry, where once some candidates were accepted on the spot because the managers need bodies to fill open spots on the floor. That was regardless of the candidate's actual potential, work background or educational credentials.

Tips for the Younger Worker

1. Be aggressive in your search. It's imperative to show off your limited skills and experience by being enthusiastic.

2. Follow instructions. Don't apply to a job

in just any random fashion. You must follow the employer's job application rules.

3. Network. In person, online and over the phone. Never stop meeting new business professionals.

4. Find a mentor. Locate someone who's successful in your industry and pursue a lunch or two. They might know someone hiring, too.

5. Get a professional resume developed. You must look and act the part of a working professional.

6. Make friends with the person who runs your school's career development center. Make sure you are aware of all new job postings and are ready to interview with any potential employers who are visiting the institution.

7. Network.

Mature Boomer

"I'm too old for this job." "Why would they hire me? I'm a dinosaur." I wish I could explain to these candidates that they shouldn't underestimate their value in today's workforce. I want to explain to them that they still need to come into the interview fired up and ready to work. Show some youthful energy. It rubs off. On top of that, experience is something you can bring to the table even if you're technically "starting over." Don't come in intimidated. Don't listen to the stigma! Don't accept "You're overqualified" or "You're accepting this job until something better comes along." These are objections you need to push past continue to demonstrate your skills and your desire to land that job.

Tips for the Older Worker

1. If you're the 40+ aged worker, make money from the experience and contacts you've built up. Target companies that won't discriminate based on how many birthday candles you had on your cake last year.

2. Please don't lead off the interview with, "I'm 45 years old. Am I too old?" Stop! During the interview, reflect your age as an attitude and as a good thing! Show your energy. If it comes down to it, maybe this job isn't the right fit for you.

3. Check *into www.ourexperiencecounts.com* for wonderful resources relating to re-entry and other obstacle killers.

4. Seek out guidance from career coaches and recruiters.

5. Learn and understand new technologies. It's important to be able to play the game as it's currently being played.

6. Brush up on your interviewing skills.

7. Don't get discouraged. It's not easy, but others are successful at it. Find them and ask how they did it.

8. Network.

Z

Zoning Into Your New Job

"Try not to become a man of success but rather to become a man of value." — Albert Einstein

Once you have actually landed a new job, it's best to keep it for a while. Job hopping is the number 1 red flag for recruiters. Someone who can last any time after three years at a job is considered a strong candidate. When you've had six jobs in the past two years, it becomes worrisome for the hiring manager. Here is a list of some tidbits for you to use to keep positive and effective at your current job.

One quick thing I want to mention. On your first day of work, don't stand out negatively. First impressions always go a long way and if this is your new job, your first impression will last a long time. It's best that your first question to your boss isn't "So when will I get paid?" or "How long do I have for lunch?" or "What are my benefits?" Those will get answered in time, so be patient and go with the flow during the first few days or weeks.

1. Email your boss or an important co-worker from home and at night! It always looks impressive when you're burning the midnight oil. So why not show them you're doing some work at night—when you actually are. If you have some ideas that come to mind about a certain project, let your superiors or colleagues know it, right then and there.

2. Be indispensable. Volunteer at the office for unpopular jobs, duties or projects. This will show that you are a team player without being a

brown-noser.

3. Go above and beyond. I know this expression is used loosely, but it's true. Do some extra research for a project. Be responsive. The more strategic you are with your job duties, the more broadly qualified you become and thus the more responsibilities you might earn. Remember, more responsibilities tend to lead to more pay.

4. It's good to get an idea of the company's overall scheme of things. Look at an organizational chart and see where you fit into the entire picture. It's good to have knowledge of your competitors, the players and how your company's market share affects your industry's overall growth. Know your business and know what's happening within your company at all times, especially within the broken economies. It's best to be prepared for anything.

5. Treat your position like a CEO. No matter what it takes, always act like you have an important job and that you take it very seriously. Managers will see this and know you're capable of much more.

6. Show, don't tell.

7. Make a mark with the bigwigs. Reach out with ideas and proposals if you think they will benefit the company. Make your own waves and work hard. Things will come your way if you do.

8. If you're a rank and file worker, work your way into management. If you're an exempt or professional worker, set your sights to become a leader or executive.

9. If your company asks you to take a pay cut, go for it if you can afford it. Ask questions such as "Is it just me or just our department?" "Could I take some stock options in lieu of the lost salary?", "When will I get the raise again to match where I

am at today?", "Is there some opportunity I can gain in my career in exchange for taking the pay cut?" Be a team player if it will still put food on the table.

10. Participate in outside work activities. Some companies create activities to make sure they have employees who can be different from regular people. That could be anything from dancing an Irish jig in front of the co-workers to leading a yoga class.

Six Steps to Avoid Underemployment

If you want to raise your salary and employment level, you need to take action. Here's what to do:

1. Figure out what you're best at and pursue that with all you've got.

2. Develop a short- and long-term goal list and do checks against those lists weekly, monthly and every three months.

3. Find a career coach or mentor and heed their expertise.

4. Train and get certified in the position you hold now. Do whatever you can to learn and become an expert.

5. Surround yourself with positive and functional people. Ensure they, too, are on the right track and display positive outlooks. Associate with other hard workers. You need to be around people like yourself. Together you can learn, grow and overcome larger obstacles.

6. Take calculated risks. Keep pushing and doing things that are hard. The harder the task, the better the payoff. You must never settle!

Appendix A

Job Links

Here are some websites to get you moving on your job searching and posting duties.

General Job Boards
www.careerbuilder.com
www.careersite.com
www.careerexposure.com
www.careerjet.com
www.craigslist.org
www.employmentguide.com
www.hotjobs.com
www.indeed.com
www.job.com
www.jobopenings.net
www.jobcentral.com
www.jobfox.com
www.jobbankinfo.org
www.jobrapido.com
www.jobster.com
www.jobofmine.com
www.jobbankusa.com
www.justjobs.com
www.linkedin.com
www.linkup.com
www.monster.com
www.myspace.com
www.simplyhired.com
www.twithire.com
www.truecareers.com

Niche Job Boards
Aerospace
www.aeroindustryjobs.com
www.ctsinternational.com

Agriculture/Forestry

www.agcareers.com
www.agindustryjobs.com
www.treecarejobs.com

Architecture
www.architecturejobs.com
www.e-architect.com

Aviation/Airline
www.avianation.com
www.aviationcrossing.com
www.aviationemployment.com
www.aviationjobsearch.com
www.avjobs.com
www.aviationemploymentboard.net
www.faa.gov/jobs

Call Center
www.callcentercareers.com
www.callcenterclassifieds.com
www.callcenterjobs.com

Child Care
www.care.com
www.greataupair.com
www.nannies4hire.com
www.nannypro.com

Communications/Media/PR/Arts/
Entertainment
www.actorsaccess.com
www.amfmjobs.com
www.artjob.org
www.artcareer.net
www.backstage.com
www.careerpage.org

www.creativejobscentral.com
www.journalismjobs.com
www.krop.com
www.lacasting.com
www.massmediajobs.com
www.mediabistro.com
www.newsjobs.com
www.nowcasting.com
www.prweekjobs.com
www.talentzoo.com
www.thebiz.variety.com
www.tvjobs.com
www.tvandradiojobs.com
www.washingtonpost.com
www.workinpr.com
www.writejobs.com

Construction/Manufacturing/Warehouse

www.constructionexecutive.com
www.constructionjobs.com
www.hvacagent.com
www.infooil.com
www.jobsinmanufacturing.com
www.justprojectmanagerjobs.com
www.manufacturingjobs.com
www.mepjobs.com
www.offshore-marine.com
www.oilandgasjobsonline.com
www.oiljobfinder.com
www.topbuildingjobs.com
www.warehousejobs.com

Contract/Temporary/Freelance/Home-Based

www.backdoorjobs.com
www.bridgestar.org
www.coolworks.com

www.elance.com
www.execsearches.com
www.gofreelance.com
www.groovejob.com
www.guru.com
www.homeworkers.org
www.ifreelance.com
www.jobsformoms.com
www.jobmonkey.com
www.net-temps.com
www.nonprofitoyster.com
www.opportunityknocks.org
www.snagajob.com
www.sologig.com
www.tides.org
www.tjobs.com
www.worldwideworkathome.com
www.xgo.co.uk

Diversity
www.diversitysearch.com
www.diversityjobs.com
www.diversityworking.com
www.hirediversity.com
www.latpro.com
www.workplacediversity.com

Education
www.eteach.com
www.higheredjobs.com
www.schoolspring.com
www.teachers-teachers.com
www.jobsmotion.com/teaching-jobs

Entry Level/Internships
www.aftercollege.com

www.campuscareercenter.com
www.collegerecruiter.com
www.collegegrad.com
www.experience.com
www.internjobs.com
www.jobweb.com
www.makingthedifference.org
www.studentjobs.gov

Environmental/Green/Energy
www.acre-resources.co.uk
www.brightgreentalent.com
www.coolclimatejobs.com
www.earthworks-jobs.com
www.ecoemploy.com
www.ecojobs.com
www.environmental-jobs.com
www.energyjobsearch.com
www.environmentalcareer.com
www.environmentjob.co.uk
www.greenbiz.com
www.greencollar.org
www.greenjobs.com
www.greendreamjobs.com
www.grist.org
www.lowcarbon.com
www.sustainjobs.com
www.stopdodo.com
www.treehugger.com
www.utility-worker.com
www.utilityjobsonline.com

Executive
www.lucasgroup.com
www.conwaygreenwood.com
www.telesolutionsearch.com

www.dmrglobal.com
www.scionstaffing.com
www.scsanantonio.com
www.csccareers.com
www.grevenandassociates.com
www.millerresource.com
www.spencerkeystone.com
www.nationalexecutivepersonnel.com
www.grosrecruiters.com
www.jmsearch.com
www.kornferry.com
www.battaliawinston.com
www.russellreynolds.com
www.diversifiedsearch.com
www.boyden.com
www.mrinetwork.com
www.heidrick.com
www.atkearney.com
Fashion/Design
www.aigadesignjobs.org
www.clothingindustryjobs.com
www.coroflot.com
www.fashioncareercenter.com
www.stylecareers.com

Finance/Banking/Accounting
www.accountingjobstoday.com
www.bankjobs.com
www.brokerhunter.com
www.careersinaudit.com
www.careersintax.com
www.careerbank.com
www.eFinancialCareers.com
www.jobsinthemoney.com
www.taxtalent.com

Fitness/Wellness

www.exercisecareers.com
www.exercisejobs.com
www.fitnessjobs.com

Government

www.apps.opm.gov/sppc_directory
www.amtrak.net
www.anl.gov
www.archives.gov
www.atf.gov
www.bnl.gov
www.borderpatrol.gov
www.bop.gov
www.brubach.com
www.cbo.gov
www.cbp.gov
www.census.gov
www.cftc.gov
www.clearancejobs.com
www.cia.gov
www.cms.hhs.gov
www.cpsc.gov
www.dcjobsource.com
www.defensetalent.com
www.dfid.gov.uk
www.dhs.gov
www.dla.mil
www.doi.gov
www.dol.gov
www.ed.gov
www.epa.gov
www.exim.gov
www.faa.gov
www.fcc.gov
www.fbijobs.gov

www.fbo.gov
www.fda.gov
www.fdic.gov
www.fec.gov
www.fedbizopps.gov
www.federalreserve.gov
www.fema.gov
www.ferc.gov
www.ftc.gov
www.fws.gov
www.gao.gov
www.gpo.gov
www.go-defense.com
www.governmentjobs.com
www.govcentral.com
www.govtjobs.com
www.hhs.govwww.house.gov
www.hud.gov
www.irs.gov
www.loc.gov
www.makingthedifference.org
www.nasa.gov
www.nationalservice.gov
www.nga.gov
www.nhtsa.dot.gov
www.nih.gov
www.nlrb.gov
www.noaa.gov
www.nps.gov
www.nrc.gov
www.nsa.gov
www.nsf.gov
www.ntsb.gov
www.opic.gov
www.opm.gov
www.ornl.gov

www.pbgc.gov
www.peacecorps.gov
www.recovery.gov
www.sealiftcommand.com
www.senate.gov
www.sihr.si.edu
www.sec.gov
www.ssa.gov
www.state.gov
www.studentjobs.gov
www.supremecourtus.gov
www.tsa.gov
www.usaid.gov
www.usajobs.gov
www.uscourts.gov
www.usda.gov
www.usdoj.gov
www.usgs.gov
www.usmint.gov
www.usps.com
www.uspto.gov
www.ustreas.gov
www.va.gov
www.wdrs.fnal.gov
www.whitehouse.gov

Hospitality/Food/Restaurant
www.caterer.com
www.fastfoodjobs.co.uk
www.foodindustryjobs.com
www.foodindustrycareers.co.uk
www.foodservice.com
www.hcareers.com
www.hsuperstars.com
www.hospitalityonline.com
www.hoteljobs.com

www.mycateringjobs.com
www.starchefsjobfinder.com

Human Resources/Recruiting
www.ere.net
www.jobs4hr.com
www.ihirehr.com
www.recruitingjobs.com
www.shrm.org
www.workforcehrjobs.com

Insurance/Underwriting
www.greatinsurancejobs.com
www.insurancejobs.com
www.ultimateinsurancejobs.com
www.underwritingjobs.com
www.insuranceunderwritingweb.com

International Development
www.aic2000.org
www.ap.urscorp.com
www.alertnet.org
www.bond.org.uk
www.careersunited.org
www.comminit.com
www.developmentaid.org
www.devex.com
www.devj.net
www.devnetjobs.org
www.dev-zone.org
www.eldis.org
www.fpa.org
www.globalrecruitment.net
www.hacesfalta.com
www.icsc.un.org
www.idealist.org

www.intljobs.org
www.internationaljobs.org
www.interaction.org
www.microfinancegateway.org
www.oneworld.net
www.overseasjobs.com
www.thirdsector.co.uk
www.tol.cz
www.uvm.edu
www.vso.org.uk

IT/Engineering
www.computerjobs.com
www.computerwork.com
www.databasejobs.com
www.dbjobs.org
www.dice.com
www.engcen.com
www.engineerjobs.com
www.engineerjobsearch.com
www.gjc.org
www.justtechjobs.com
www.prgjobs.com
www.tech-centric.net
www.theitjobboard.com

Law
www.attorneyjobs.com
www.emplawyernet.com
www.lawcrossing.com
www.lawjobs.com

Law Enforcement
www.911hotjobs.com
www.lawenforcementjobs.com
www.policeemployment.com

Leisure
www.leisurejobs.com

Linguists
www.jobsmotion.com/all-jobs/multilingual-jobs

www.toplanguagejobs.co.uk

Logistics/Distribution/Drivers
www.classadrivers.com
www.everytruckjob.com
www.jobsinlogistics.com
www.jobsintrucks.com
www.jobsinmanufacturing.com
www.maritimejobs.com
www.supplychainjobs.com

MBAs/Executives
www.6figurejobs.com
www.execsearches.com
www.execunet.com
www.MBACareers.com
www.theladders.com

Medical/Bio/Pharmaceutical/Healthcare
www.biohealthmatics.com
www.biospace.com
www.careerpharm.com
www.globalhealth.org
www.healthcareerweb.com
www.healthecareers.com
www.healthjobsusa.com
www.hospitaljobsonline.com
www.medhunters.com
www.medicalworkers.com

www.medzilla.com
www.pharmadiversityjobboard.com
www.practicematch.com
www.rxcareercenter.com
www.therapyjobs.com

Military
www afcrossroads.com
www armypays.com
www.army.mil
www.corporategrayonline.com
www.defensetalent.com
www.destinygrp.com
www.hireahero.org
www.marineea.org
www.militaryjobzone.com
www.militarystars.com
www.militarycandidates.com
www.military.com
www.military.com/spouse
www.moaa.org
www.recruitmilitary.com
www.taonline.com
www.uscg.mil
www.va.gov
www.vetjobs.com

Mining
www.miningjobs.org
www.minejob.com
www.miscojobs.com

Non-Profit/Volunteer
www.alertnet.org
www.backdoorjobs.com
www.charityjob.co.uk

www.idealist.org
www.nonprofitjobs.org
www.nonprofit-jobs.org
www.opportunitynocs.org
www.reliefweb.int
www.unjobs.org
www.volunteermatch.org

Nursing
www.allnurses.com
www.expedientmedstaff.com
www.jobsmotion.com/nursing-jobs
www.nursingjobs.com
www.nursingjobs.org
www.nursing-jobs.us

Retail
www.allretailjobs.com
www.clothingindustryjobs.com
www.fashioncareercenter.com

Retirees
www.retirementjobs.com
www.retireandconsult.com
www.seniorjobbank.org

Sales/Marketing/Advertising
www.acareerinsales.com
www.jobs4sales.com
www.marketingjobs.com
www.salesjobs.com
www.salesheads.com
www.salestrax.com
www.talentzoo.com
www.topsalespositions.com

Science
www.nature.com
www.sciencejobs.org
www.scjobs.sciencemag.org

Security
www.clearancejobs.com
www.clearedconnections.com
www.securityjobs.net

Sports
www.jobsinsports.com
www.sportscareerfinder.com
www.teamworkonline.com
www.workinsports.com

Telecommunications
www.tech-centric.net
www.telecomcareers.net
www.wirelessjobs.com

www.ingramcontent.com/pod-product-compliance
Lightning Source LLC
Chambersburg PA
CBHW051646170526
45167CB00001B/347